A THOUSAND
SHALL FALL

To order additional copies of *A Thousand Shall Fall*,
by Susi Hasel Mundy, call 1-800-765-6955.
Visit us at www.reviewandherald.com for information on other
Review and Herald products.

A THOUSAND SHALL FALL

THE ELECTRIFYING STORY OF A SOLDIER AND HIS FAMILY
WHO DARED TO PRACTICE THEIR FAITH IN HITLER'S GERMANY

Susi Hasel Mundy

with Maylan Schurch

REVIEW AND HERALD® PUBLISHING ASSOCIATION
HAGERSTOWN, MD 21740

The author assumes full responsibility for the accuracy of all facts
and quotations as cited in this book.

Texts credited to NIV are from the *Holy Bible, New International Version.* Copyright
© 1973, 1978, 1984, International Bible Society. Used by permission of Zondervan
Bible Publishers.
Bible texts credited to RSV are from the Revised Standard Version of the Bible,
copyright © 1946, 1952, 1971, by the Division of Christian Education of the National
Council of the Churches of Christ in the U.S.A. Used by permission.

This book was
Edited by Andy Nash
Cover designed by Willie S. Duke
Background cover photo by AP Photo
Interior design by Madelyn Ruiz
Electronic makeup by Shirley M. Bolivar
Typeset:: 11/12.5 Bembo

PRINTED IN U.S.A.

07 06   9 8

R&H Cataloging Service
Mundy, Heide-Traude Susi Hasel, 1943-
    A thousand shall fall

    1. Hasel, Franz Josef, 1899-1991.   2. Hasel, Maria Magdalena, 1903-1985.
3. World War II, 1939-1945—Biography.   4. Germany—1933-1945—Biography

[B]

ISBN-10: 0-8280-1561-9
ISBN-13: 978-0-8280-1561-5

DEDICATION

To the memory of Gerhard (1935-1994),

who encouraged me to write this book.

CONTENTS

Europe during World War II

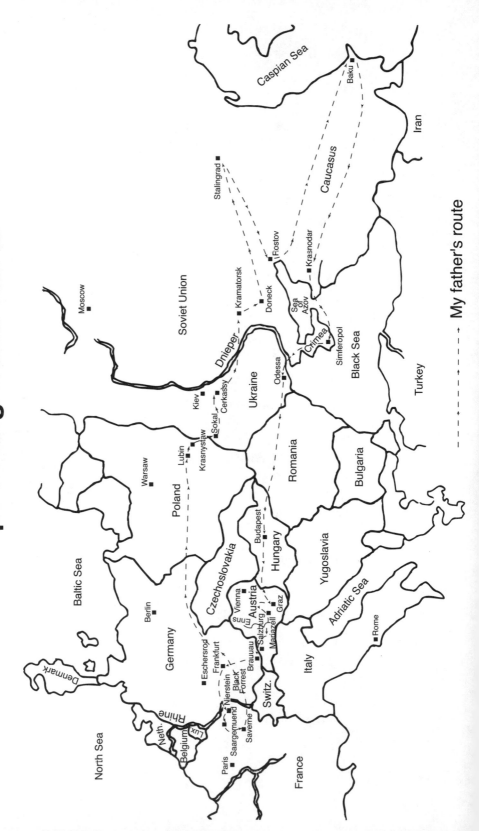

My father's route

TO THE READER

This is the story of my family during World War II. The account is based on the recollections of the participants. In writing and on tapes my parents recorded the events in meticulous detail. My brothers and sister have told me their memories.

I should mention, however, that I have taken certain liberties in the telling of the story, particularly having to do with the precise sequence of events and who may have said what to whom. Also, I have sometimes combined two or more people into one when I felt it necessary for clarification and simplification. Nevertheless, my intention was always to illuminate more brightly the truth.

It is my hope that this book will be an encouragement to God's people during the time of the end.

A Mighty Fortress Is Our God

by Martin Luther

A mighty fortress is our God,
A bulwark never failing;
Our helper He, amid the flood
Of mortal ills prevailing.
For still our ancient foe
Doth seek to work us woe;
His craft and power are great;
And armed with cruel hate,
On earth is not his equal.

Did we in our own strength confide,
Our striving would be losing,
Were not the right man on our side,
The man of God's own choosing.
Dost ask who that may be?
Christ Jesus, it is He,
Lord Sabaoth His name,
From age to age the same,
And He must win the battle.

And though this world, with devils filled,
Should threaten to undo us,
We will not fear, for God hath willed
His truth to triumph through us.
The prince of darkness grim,
We tremble not for him;
His rage we can endure,
For lo! His doom is sure,
One little word shall fell him.

That word above all earthly powers,
No thanks to them, abideth;
The Spirit and the gifts are ours
Through Him who with us sideth;
Let goods and kindred go,
This mortal life also;
The body they may kill;
God's truth abideth still,
His kingdom is forever.

CHAPTER 1

THE DRAFT

Nobody, *nobody*, can defeat us!"

Chin held high, the teacher gazed into the solemn faces of his third-grade students.

The year was 1939, and most of his fellow Frankfurt citizens shared the teacher's confidence. After all, hadn't their Fatherland and their Führer proved this over the past two decades? German hard work, German quality-control, and German stubbornness had lifted them from war-blasted paupers to Europe's most energetic nation. The future belonged to the Reich.

"We are the strongest people on earth," he told his class. "And best of all, children, if anyone should dare to invade our airspace, we have the Flak cannons."

Nine-year-old Kurt Hasel sat straighter. He pressed his lips together and took a breath through his nose.

"These cannons are located all over Germany," the teacher said. "They are so precisely calibrated that they can shoot any airplane out of the sky. This is why Germany will be victorious!"

Kurt's gaze wandered proudly to the window. Through it he could see the sun sparkling on Frankfurt's sturdy green trees. This was his Germany, his Fatherland, the greatest country in the world.

"Mutti," he said to his mother that evening, "won't it be wonderful to win the war?"

Mother cupped a hand around each of his shoulders and turned him to face her. "Kurt."

"What?"

Her voice was serious. "I want you to remember something."

He tried to wriggle away, but she held him firmly.

"Kurt, if we win the war, it means that we have taken other peoples' countries away from them."

"So?"

"Millions of people will lose their homes and their lives." Her hand loosened from his shoulders, her arms went around him, and her voice spoke from just above his dark head. "Children will be separated from their parents and their brothers and sisters. You might never see Gerd and Lotte again." She squeezed him and gave him a little shake. "War is wrong, Kurt. Killing is wrong. God wants the Hasels to be peacemakers."

"Still," Kurt said stubbornly, his voice muffled against her, "it would be exciting to see airplanes being shot out of the sky."

By 1939 Franz and Helene Hasel and their neighbors knew that Adolf Hitler was indeed preparing for war. And like everybody else, the little Seventh-day Adventist family had been wondering what the future would hold.

They were soon to find out.

One warm Sabbath after church, they entered the lobby of their suburban apartment building.

Six-year-old Lotte darted over to the Hasel mailbox and looked through the slot. "Mail, Papa," she said.

Franz unlocked the box and took out a bundle of letters. Flipping through them, he said, "Only business mail. It can wait till after sundown."

Helene quickly heated up the customary Sabbath meal consisting of dark bread and the lentil soup she had prepared the day before.

"Please, can we go to the Bird Paradise?" Kurt begged. "It's so nice today."

Lotte and 4-year-old Gerhard (the family nicknamed him Gerd) chimed in. "Please? Please, Papa?"

Franz gave one longing glance at a stack of books on his desk. He liked to study the Bible and Ellen White's writings and had been looking forward to a quiet afternoon at home. He sighed and nodded.

The walk soon led them away from civilization and into the wide expanse of open fields that stretched behind their large apartment complex. The children delighted in walking on the narrow trails through the ripening fields. Sky-blue cornflowers and scarlet poppies peeped through the still-faintly-green wheat shafts, which stood taller than their heads.

"Let's pretend we're the children of Israel," Kurt said. "We're walking through the sea. Those flowers are the fish."

Eventually, the family reached a railway embankment. Carefully crossing the narrow footbridge that spanned it, they listened to the faint humming of the rails far below. On the other side they rested on the warm grass.

"A train!" Lotte called out.

As the passenger cars roared and clicked their way along the tracks below, little Gerd clung to mother's skirt while Kurt and Lotte waved to the engineer and the smiling passengers. This time the friendly driver even blew the train's whistle for them. It was a red-letter day—one the children would remember as their last day of untroubled happiness for several years.

As the train disappeared, the family wandered down a sandy path that followed the tracks until they reached the place they called the Bird Paradise. It was like a secret garden surrounded by a thick, high hedge. There was no gate, and no eye could penetrate the green thicket. But the most melodious bird songs floated out of that mysterious place.

Helene and Franz sat down in the shade of the hedge and quietly discussed the threatening political climate. Lotte started picking wild flowers while Kurt and Gerd collected pretty pebbles and snail shells. When a cool evening breeze started blowing, they wended their way home.

After supper and sundown worship Franz got the stack of mail.

"All right, let's see who's sending us letters," he said. He dealt them on the kitchen table into piles.

Suddenly he paused, peering closely at an official-looking envelope.

"Helene. It can't be. But I think—"

He slit one end of the envelope and drew out a stiff piece of folded paper. Helene looked over his shoulder.

"That's impossible," she said. "You're 40 years old. There's some mistake."

Franz's voice, usually so confident, now sounded dazed and thick. "It is. It's a letter from the draft board. I am summoned to the army recruitment center in Frankfurt on Monday at 8:00 a.m."

"This Monday?"

"This Monday. In two days."

Helene and Franz stared at each other.

"I thought I was too old," he said. "Instead, it looks like I'm one of the first to be called up."

He herded the children into the living room and told them to sit down. Then he explained that he had been called to be a soldier.

Lotte started crying. "Soldiers get killed in war," she sobbed. "Will you die?"

Franz opened his mouth to reply, but before he had a chance to say anything, Kurt said scornfully, "Don't be silly, Lotte. Germany is the strongest country in the world. The other soldiers will die, not ours."

"Papa won't die?" Lotte asked hopefully.

"Of course not," Kurt replied. "We have powerful weapons that no one can defeat. And we have the Flak antiaircraft artillery that can shoot airplanes out of the sky if they attack us. We will win the war, and Papa will be a hero, and Germany will rule the whole world."

Franz's face turned white. A devout Seventh-day Adventist, he was firmly pacifist. He hadn't suspected how fully his firstborn son, at age 9, had bought into Hitler's goal to make Germany the center of an expanding 1,000-year "Third Reich" superpower.

"Kurt. Children. Listen to me."

Gerd climbed on Papa's lap and started sucking his thumb. Franz tried to explain why war was wrong and that Hitler was a bad man who did not love God. Kurt listened, but the jut of his small jaw showed that he still thought that being a soldier would be a jolly good adventure.

Monday at the recruitment center Franz passed his physical exam. Then he filled out a lengthy information sheet and handed it to the officer in charge.

"Sir," he said politely, "I am a Seventh-day Adventist Christian and a conscientious objector. I would like to serve as a medic."

The officer looked him over. "Seventh-day Adventist," he repeated. "Never heard of it." He called across the room to a colleague. "Hey, Hans. Do you know anything about Seventh-day Adventists?"

"They are like the Jews," Hans yelled back. "They keep Sabbath."

The officer gave Franz a baleful look. "Well then," he finally said, "what would you do if you were caring for a wounded soldier and the enemy launched an attack?"

"I would lie on top of the man and shield him with my body, sir."

"Indeed!" The officer rolled his eyes, then said spitefully, "Well, we have no room for cowards in the German army." He flipped through some papers, then wrote Franz's appointment on the intake form. Franz had been assigned to serve as a private in Pioneer Park Company 699.

Franz swallowed. He knew the Pioneers well—at age 18 he had served with them in World War I. The Pioneers were engineering units that prepared the way for the army to follow. He also knew that the prestigious Company 699 was assigned the task of building bridges wherever Hitler planned his next advance.

This means, Franz thought to himself, *that the soldiers in 699 will always be among the first Germans in enemy territory. No doubt the officer had put him on the front lines because he hated men who were not supportive of Hitler's war effort.*

"Don't just stand there, private," the officer snapped. "Move on. We have other people to process."

Franz went to the clothing barracks, where he was issued the complete gray-green uniform of the German army. He received a pair of trousers and a combat tunic with four patch pockets, gold tresses on the collar, and the emblem of the Nazi eagle clutching the swastika sewn above the right breast pocket. He also received a wide black leather belt, from which he could hang his bread bag with provisions. He was given a pair of shoes, a pair of high boots, a side hat, a steel helmet, and underwear and socks.

He was told to report to duty on Wednesday morning.

Back home, the children explored the uniform. Lotte liked to carry her dolly in the bread bag. The various compartments were just right for a spare bottle and diapers.

Gerd put on the side hat with the colorful red dot in front encircled by a white and black ring.

Kurt cocked his finger and aimed it at Gerd. "Bang! I hit you right in the forehead. You're dead!" Gerd promptly started to cry.

But Kurt's favorite was the steel helmet. He liked the smell of the new leather webbing that lined its crown. Padding it with newspaper to keep it from sliding over his eyes, he proudly paraded through the house proclaiming that no one could hurt him.

In the next couple of days Franz had much do to. For years he had been a literature evangelist and publishing secretary in Austria and Germany. So now he contacted the publishing house in Hamburg and the conference president to inform them he'd been drafted. Working methodically, he finished reports and answered letters so that when he left, his work would all be in order.

On Wednesday morning Franz buttoned and buckled his uniform on, then called the family together. Lotte looked at him with awe, and whispered, "Oh, Papa, you are so handsome!"

Kurt studied the belt buckle: the Nazi eagle encircled by the words Gott Mit Uns, meaning "God With Us."

"Papa," he said thoughtfully, "if Hitler wants God to be with us, he can't be that bad."

"Kurt," Franz said with intensity. "Hitler is an evil man. Never trust what he says. You stay true to God and God only! But come now, let's have worship before I have to leave."

Franz read from Psalm 91:5-11 "Thou shalt not be afraid for the terror by night; nor for the arrow that flieth by day; . . . a thousand shall fall at thy side, and ten thousand at thy right hand; but it shall not come nigh thee. . . . For he shall give his angels charge over thee, to keep thee in all thy ways."

Then the family sang their favorite hymn, "A Mighty Fortress Is Our God." Afterward they knelt in a circle and held hands while Franz prayed.

"Our Father," he said, "I have been drafted to be a soldier. You know that I have no interest in war and in fighting. You know that I found no joy in battle in the Great War, even when I wasn't a Christian yet. Much less so, now.

"Please be with us, Father, as our paths separate. Help me to be true to my faith even in the army. Help me so that I will not have to kill anyone. Please bring me back safely, and protect my family from all the dangers of war at home. Amen."

It was getting late. They quickly said their good-byes, and Franz left, feeling in his heart that one day they all would be back together again.

CHAPTER 2

IN BOOT CAMP

A near-carnival atmosphere reigned in Frankfurt's central train station. Two hundred soldiers in smart new uniforms were being sent to boot camp in Nierstein on the banks of the Rhine River. Clean-shaven, sporting new haircuts, standing proudly in their crisp uniforms, they looked strong and confident.

Wives and sweethearts hugged their men. A few were crying, but most were in a holiday mood, waving blood-red swastikas and scattering confetti. A group in the center of the crowd drank champagne and sang victory songs.

Awkwardly the soldiers held bouquets of flowers and fancily-wrapped boxes of chocolates given them by the women. A young lady Franz had never seen before kissed him on both cheeks and wished him good luck. Finally the train steamed out of the station to the thunderous roar of the German's battle cry: *"Ein Volk, ein Reich, ein Führer! Sieg Heil!* Sieg Heil!" One People, One Empire, One Leader! Victory Salvation! Victory Salvation!

A muted shock coursed through Franz. *Hitler's demonic power of suggestion has captured the masses,* he thought. *They're convinced that the war will be over by Christmas, and that Germany will soon rule a better world.*

As the train pulled away from the station, he started chatting with some of the others. He hit it off especially well with a Karl Hoffman, and the two men initiated a friendship.

Three hours later they arrived in Nierstein, where the new recruits settled into their quarters while the rest of their battalion arrived, 1,200 men in all. The bridge-building Pioneer Park Company 699 was one of Hitler's elite troops who took orders directly from headquarters in Berlin. Many of the men were skilled craftsmen and mechanics.

On Friday Franz searched out the Hauptmann (captain) of his unit, a man named Brandt. He found him in a room talking with his accountant and a clerk. He had a pleasant expression on his face.

"Herr Hauptmann," Franz said, "may I have permission to present two requests?"

"Speak out, man. What are they?"

"As you know, sir, I am a Seventh-day Adventist. I worship God on Saturday as the Bible teaches us to do. I would like to be excused from reporting for duty on my Sabbath day. Also, I do not eat pork or anything else that comes from pigs. I respectfully request permission to receive a substitute whenever pork products are being served."

Taken by surprise, the Hauptmann was at a loss how to respond. Behind him, the accountant and the clerk glanced at each other, rolled their eyes to the ceiling, and tapped their foreheads.

Finally, Hauptmann Brandt shrugged. "If you can work the details out with the lieutenant, I am agreeable."

Franz looked for Lieutenant Peter Gutschalk, a surly man who had already earned the nickname Seltenfroehlich—"Seldomcheerful."

Saluting smartly, Franz repeated his requests.

Gutschalk's face turned beet red. "You must be mad, private!" he bellowed. "This is the German army! This battalion's going to war, and you want Saturday off?" Under his breath he spat out, "It's just my luck to be saddled with a religious nut!"

"I just want permission," Franz said mildly, "to trade work with other soldiers so that my free day falls on Saturday."

Gasping for air like a goldfish, the lieutenant roared, "Get out of my sight!"

Franz began to back away.

"Work out whatever you want," the officer continued. "But let me tell you this, Hasel. Once the advance starts, the war is not going to come to a standstill just so you can keep your Sabbath! Furthermore, if I see you shirking your duty in any way, I will personally see that you will live to regret it! Remember, I have my eye on you!"

When Franz got back to the barracks, he asked the men if they would swap Sunday duty with him. His new friend, Karl Hoffman, immediately agreed, and there were other takers, too. Special entertainment and dances were planned for Sundays, and since local girls admired the uniformed men, who knew what romances could develop?

Encouraged by his success, Franz made his way to the kitchen. There he explained his dietary principles to the head cook and asked if he could have a substitute whenever pork was served.

The cook put his hands on his hips and stared Franz up and down.

"Private Hasel," he said tensely, a Lieutenant Gutschalk-like flush beginning to creep up his neck above his collar, "let me just educate you about our diet. For breakfast we serve bread, jam, and coffee. For lunch we serve stew. For supper we serve bread and sausage or other meat, and sometimes cheese. Also, four times a week you get two ounces of butter in the evening and three times a week two ounces of lard."

As he talked, the cook became more and more infuriated. "You know, Hasel, you really have nerve! This is the army, not a gourmet cookery that caters to special wishes."

He rapped his knuckles on a giant kettle, which gave forth a booming ring. "See this? I have one kettle. All the food gets cooked in it. You'll eat what everyone eats, or for all I care, you can starve! Pork, indeed!" He stared closely at Franz's face. "I believe you are a disguised Jew. Just you wait, we'll find you out!"

Later as Franz went through the supper line, the cook insolently slapped an extra large portion of sausage onto his plate.

Franz stared down at the rich, gristly meat. Should he eat what the Lord had forbidden or should he just eat the bread and go hungry? Later, back in the barracks, he turned to the book of Daniel and reread the story of the three faithful youths who would not touch the king's food. Then and there he recommitted himself to be faithful to the Lord's dietary guidelines.

But he needed his nourishment, so something had to be done.

At that time Franz, along with 30 other soldiers, was billeted in a house located across the street from a dairy store. On Monday morning he paid a visit to the owner.

"I am going to be stationed here for some time and would like to set up a bartering system with you," he said. "Would you be interested in trading dairy products for pork?"

"Of course," the woman replied, delighted to get access to some of the Pioneer's delicacies. They bartered a bit, and finally she said, "I'll give you a liter of milk per day and a quarter of a pound of butter every third day in return for your portions of pork, lard, and sausage."

Every morning thereafter Franz broke his coarse army bread into little pieces, put them into his bowl, doused everything with fresh dairy milk, and ate it with a spoon. The other soldiers started to get jealous of his seemingly unlimited supply of milk and butter.

"Hey, Carrot Eater," they said. "You're living pretty high, aren't you?"

Franz grinned good-naturedly. "You just go ahead and eat your pigs. I prefer this."

"That's all fine and good," they responded, "but what are you going to do when we get to the front and can't trade any more?"

"I'm not worrying about it. God will take care of me."

And indeed, the company was in hard training for frontline action. In addition to taking basic army instruction, the Pioneers built several bridges across the Rhine River. It was hard, backbreaking work. At noon, the field kitchen brought the food to the building site. When Franz looked in the kettle and saw pork, he took no food at all. He always carried extra bread and cheese along and ate that instead.

Once a soldier from another company noticed this.

"Say," he said, "I notice you eat no meat. Is there a reason?"

Franz explained his convictions.

"Well, we've got a guy in our company who doesn't eat pork either."

"Really? Where is he? What's his name?"

"Michel. I don't remember his last name."

"It wouldn't be Michel Schroedel?"

"That's the name!" The soldier pointed. "He works in that building over there."

Franz ran over to the building and bounded up the steps. Inside he discovered his old friend, Michel Schroedel, the manager of the printing press at Marienhoehe Adventist Seminary. The two men had known each other for 15 years. During the four weeks before their companies separated, Franz and Michel worshipped together and encouraged each other every Sabbath.

So for the time being, two problems had been solved—Sabbath keeping and diet. Another one still remained.

Franz had become an Adventist at age 20, and had since made it a habit to read the Bible through once a year. Though he knew it wouldn't be easy, he resolved to continue this practice in the army. Every morning and evening he sat on his cot reading his Bible and praying.

The soldiers went out of their way to disrupt his devotions by telling jokes followed by bursts of raucous laughter, or by throwing shoes and pillows at him. Soon he had earned the nickname "Bible Reader" as well as "Carrot Eater."

Of all the men, Lieutenant Gutschalk was the most merciless in his ridicule. He missed no chance to humiliate Franz in front of his comrades. Franz realized that if he were to keep the respect of the men, he would have to get the better of the officer. So he began to form a plan.

One morning as they were assembling for roll call, the lieutenant asked, "Well, Hasel, have you had your worship yet?"

Franz saluted smartly. "Yes, sir."

"How can you believe such fairy tales in our enlightened times? You must be soft in the head!"

"It's interesting, Lieutenant, but I just read about people like you in 2 Peter 3:3." Franz whipped out his pocket-size Bible, opened it, and read:

" 'First of all, you must understand that in the last days scoffers will come, scoffing and following their own evil desires.' "

"This verse," said Franz, "was written more than 1,900 years ago. Thank you, sir, for confirming that the Bible is true and for strengthening my faith."

During supper a few days later, Lieutenant Gutschalk was striding along the opposite side of the dining room.

"Well, Mr. Holy Man," he called across the heads of the soldiers, "did you read anything useful in your Bible today?"

"Yes, sir," Franz shouted back, "in fact I read about you."

"About me?"

Out came Franz's little Bible. "Listen to Ecclesiastes 12:13, 14: 'Let us hear the conclusion of the whole matter: Fear God, and keep his commandments; for this is the whole duty of man, even of Lieutenant Gutschalk.' "

The soldiers whistled and applauded while Gutschalk retreated in haste. He never asked about Franz's devotions again. But he remained Franz's enemy, and continued to look for opportunities to get him into trouble.

At the end of September the Pioneers received orders to build a pontoon bridge across the Rhine River at Oppenheim. It was their first opportunity to put their training to work. They commandeered a number of river barges, reimbursing the owners. The barges were anchored together and the bridge built across them. It was a huge success. In honor of their Hauptmann, the bridge was named Brandtbruecke ("Brandt's Bridge").

When it was finished, there was a grand celebration. Flags snapped in the wind, the army band played, and Hauptmann Brandt gave a rousing speech about the high German ideals, which would soon set the standard for the whole world. The banks of the Rhine echoed with the cries of *"Ein Volk, ein Reich, ein Führer! Sieg Heil! Sieg Heil!"*

Then soldiers and townspeople crossed the Rhine on the new bridge, its wooden boards smelling of pine and still oozing pitch. Towering over each end was a German eagle clutching a swastika. This bridge survived the entire war, and was used in the fall of 1944 during the Americans' first invasion of Germany.

As the boot camp training continued, it soon became apparent that Franz was especially good at target practice and hit the bull's eye much of the time. Soon he won the admiration of others and became known as the sharpshooter of the company.

On the range one day, his friend Karl Hoffman asked, "Franz, what's the secret of your good aim?"

Franz shrugged. "I don't know that I do anything really special. I just look through the scope at the target, then point the gun a little lower and pull the trigger."

"I'm going to practice your trick. It'll probably save my life someday."

In one sense, of course, what Karl said was true. But the conversation scared Franz. When he was alone, he often wondered what he would do if an enemy attacked him. Would he instinctively reach for his gun and kill to protect himself? He remembered his promise to God not to take another man's life, yet at this point he didn't trust himself if put to the test.

Pioneer Park Company 699 celebrated their first Christmas in the army with a candlelight service in Oppenheim's majestic old cathedral along the Rhine River. The soldiers were disappointed that the war hadn't ended yet, but Hitler's rousing Christmas Eve radio address restored their confidence. Once again his hypnotic personality swayed the masses. *All is well . . . the Third Reich will soon be established . . . Germany will reign supreme for 1,000 years.*

A big party had been planned for later in the evening. Franz asked if he could stay in his quarters. No, attendance was mandatory. When he reached the meeting hall, Lieutenant Gutschalk stood at the door.

"Hasel, what are you carrying there?"

"As you know, lieutenant, I don't drink alcohol. I have here a bottle of grape juice so I can have something to drink."

"Get on in there, then," the Lieutenant grunted as he let Franz pass.

Inside the hall, long trestle tables were covered with white bed sheets and decorated with fresh spruce boughs and candles. The fragrance of the evergreens mingled with the spicy smell of the brown Christmas cakes set at each soldier's place.

The festivities started with the singing of some of the grand old German Christmas carols: *"Es Ist ein Ros' Entsprungen," "O Tannenbaum,"* and of course *"Stille Nacht."*

But soon the beer and brandy took effect, and the mood lightened. One of the soldiers had composed a poem about the characteristics of the men in the company. Franz curiously waited to see what would be said about him. Finally, it came:

"Hasel gladly reads his Bible, full of zeal as we all saw,
  Eats fresh greens and boiled potatoes, cucumbers and carrots raw.
  And he preaches to all people the good word on temperance,
  Don't eat meat, don't smoke, don't drink—that should be the Christian's stance."

He knew then that in spite of their teasing they had accepted him.

After two hours, Franz was the only sober man in the whole company. As the party became rowdier and the jokes coarser, he left the hall and spent the rest of the evening in his quarters reading his Bible.

The next day, while carrying out an order, he ran into the major and the Hauptmann. Saluting smartly, he tried to pass, but they stopped him.

"Hasel," the major said, "we noticed that you stayed sober last night. We want you to know that we appreciate that very much."

A few days later, Franz was promoted to Private First Class. To his surprise, he also received a medal, the Kriegsverdienstkreuz 2. Klasse Mit Schwertern, the War Merit Cross 2nd Class With Swords. Curiously he stared at the satin-lined box. In it gleamed the Maltese Cross with the Swastika in the center and two swords crossed diagonally, all hanging from the ribbon bar with its red, white, and black stripes and another pair of crossed swords.

He had no idea what he had done to earn this honor. In an alcohol-soaked army, sobriety alone wouldn't merit this award.

Along with his promotion came a new and unexpected benefit. Franz was relieved of all outdoor work and was appointed to be night guard in the company office. One night he again grew curious about his medal, and decided to check his file.

He found it in a file cabinet, turned to the records about the medal, and discovered that he had received the commendation "for good moral influence on the men in the entire company." He thought back over the many times he had said, "Comrades, stop your immoral talk and your dirty jokes. Don't make light of sex; sex is something sacred. Remember your wives and daughters at home. How would they feel if they heard your lewd talk?" Franz had thought that his admonitions had been spoken into the wind. Now he realized that he had been heard and appreciated.

By now, the men of the Pioneer Park Company 699 had bonded and had settled into a comfortable routine. But it was not to last.

CHAPTER 3

POLITICAL PRESSURES AT HOME

Back in Frankfurt, things got worse for Helene and the children. The food and clothing they needed were strictly rationed, and could be bought only if Helene turned in the appropriate ration cards. Everyone received one potato and two slices of bread per day, and children got one pint of milk. Later, at Christmas, there was one orange, and at Easter time, everybody would be entitled to one egg. Every six months a can of ham was provided, and every spring, each child was given a pair of shoes.

Still, morale stayed high. Hitler had started invading neighboring countries without much opposition, and Germans optimistically hoped that the war would soon be over.

Kurt and Lotte both attended the Ludwig Richter Schule. Kurt loved school—mainly because it was there that he heard thrilling daily news of Hitler's progress. His teacher told of Germany's fleet of submarines and warships, the airplanes, the bombs, the tanks, and a wonderful new "secret weapon" Hitler was developing.

Helene, however, soon had to deal with threats to her beliefs that were much more serious than the brainwashing Lotte and Kurt got in school.

The Nazionalsozialistische Deutsche Arbeiterpartei, the National Socialist German Workers Party, had become very strong—and now dominated German politics. People felt it an honor to be a Nazi, as its members were called. And party members were given many privileges, including greater rations and jobs if they wanted them. Yet Helene knew that she could never embrace Nazi ideals.

However, it wasn't easy to stay on the opposite side. In stores and public places people knew immediately where your loyalties lay by whether you used the new German greeting, *"Heil Hitler"* (Salvation to Hitler), while raising your arm. If you continued to use the traditional *"Guten Morgen"* or *"Guten Tag,"* you were thought of as disloyal to your country. Helene refused to buckle under the pressure.

One evening she answered a knock on the door. There stood Herr Doering, a neighbor who had become a party official.

"Heil Hitler," he greeted her, saluting with outstretched arm.

"Good evening," Helene replied cautiously.

"May I come in a moment?"

Silently, Helene opened the door and led him to the living room.

"Frau Hasel," he began, "we have noticed that you are not yet a member of our party. Over the years, I have observed that you and your husband have been exemplary citizens. You are the kind of people we want to be Nazis. I have been sent here to extend an invitation to you to join the party."

Helene looked at him with her clear blue eyes as he explained the benefits she would be entitled to as a party member.

"Rations will be doubled," he said. "Your children will receive not one but two pairs of shoes a year, two sets of clothes, and a warm coat for winter. You and your children will get a six-week vacation at a summer resort in the mountains or at the sea, with unrationed food. You can eat all you want."

"Lord," she silently prayed, "what am I to do here? If I don't join, I will alienate this man and endanger the lives of my little children and myself. Maybe this is a time where it would be well to outwardly comply like Queen Esther and remain true to my faith in my heart. Give me wisdom."

Herr Doering finished his appeal, put a party application and a pen into her hand, and looked at her expectantly.

Helene handed them back. "Herr Doering," she said, "my husband has been at the front since the first day of the war. I notice that the men who are party members are still here. I don't want to join a party like that. Besides, I already belong to a party."

"What party would that be?" he asked with disdain.

"It's the party of Jesus Christ. I need no other!" Helene responded.

Herr Doering seemed stunned at her daring. Then the color of humiliation rose to his cheeks. "We'll see about that!" he hissed through clenched teeth. Stomping out of the room, he slammed the apartment door behind him.

From that day, he was Helene's enemy. Though he knew that she was a Seventh-day Adventist, he began spreading the rumor that she was a Jew, which would cause her much difficulty as the war went on. Often he rang her doorbell at midnight while beating with his fists on the door. With pounding heart Helene would open it, thinking it was the Gestapo out on a midnight raid to arrest her. But there stood Herr Doering.

"Tomorrow night," he would growl, "your children will be taken from you unless you join the party."

Sometimes Helene and the children hid in a neighbor's apartment until she thought it was safe again at home. Other times she ignored the midnight racket while the terrified children hid under their beds.

Months passed. Disillusioned, the Germans were forced to recognize that the conflict was going to take longer than expected. Still, they felt that victory was certain.

Living conditions got worse. Since more and more men were being drafted, farms became less productive, and food grew scarce even with ration cards.

In public, each Jew was now required to wear a bright yellow star pinned to his or her clothing or displayed on a black armband. No longer were they permitted in movie theaters, concert halls, or even public parks. In grocery stores they were served last—if at all. And Germans who were friendly with Jews were denounced as unpatriotic.

Frau Holling was a neighbor who had lived in the Hasels' apartment building for years. Her husband was a soldier, and she was well liked and respected. One morning as Helene left the house to go to the grocery store, she saw Frau Holling with a shopping bag and waited for her. With shock she noticed the yellow star pinned to her coat. Helene hadn't realized that Frau Holling was Jewish.

"Good morning," Helene greeted her cheerfully. "I see you are going shopping, too. Let's go together."

As the two passed Herr Doering's living room window, Helene saw the lace curtain open a crack, then close again. Her fraternizing with a Jew had been duly observed.

"Oh, Frau Hasel," Frau Holling began, "I don't know how things can continue. The neighbors who have been friendly to me for years won't even greet me anymore, much less speak to me. In the grocery store they won't serve me until all Aryans have left. Sometimes I have to wait outside for hours—and then I am given the worst of the produce. Often they won't sell me anything."

"Listen," Helene said, "I have a plan. You tell me what you need and give me your ration cards, and I will buy your things for you while you wait around the corner so they don't see you."

Frau Holling swallowed. "Frau Hasel, you can't do that. It is dangerous for you to even talk to me. If you are found out, you are lost."

"I am a believer," said Helene simply. "God is able to protect His children. That includes both you and me."

"I will never forget your kindness," Frau Holling said fervently. "Now I know who my true friends are."

From then on, Helene bought Frau Holling's groceries as well as her own.

One evening a few weeks later, Helene heard a soft tap on the door. Frau Holling stood there in tears. Quickly, Helene pulled her inside.

"What has happened? Have you had news of your husband?"

"Oh, Frau Hasel," the woman sobbed. "A friend of mine has discovered that I will be arrested soon and sent to a concentration camp. I have stored my furniture with friends. If I am taken, and if my husband comes back, please tell him what happened to me."

Weeping, the two women embraced. Then Frau Holling stole out of the apartment.

The next morning as Helene scrubbed the stone stairs of the landing, she heard some neighbor women talking.

"The Gestapo came last night and arrested Frau Holling," said one. "She was shipped to Theresienstadt."

"It's just as well," someone else said. "We don't want enemies of the country around."

Then they lowered their voices, and in whispers continued their conversation. Helene looked at them, and saw that they were casting significant glances in her direction.

After the war, Frau Holling would return. The Theresienstadt camp had been liberated just days before she had been slated for execution. Once she was back in her old neighborhood, her neighbors—afraid that she would denounce them—went out of their way to be friendly to her. But she refused to have anything to do with them.

Frankfurt began to feel poverty's pinch even more painfully. In the fall, after the farmers had harvested their potatoes, Helene got permission to glean the fields for what was left. Every day after school, she took the children and the little ladder-sided handcart and went to the fields to dig up the tiny cherry-sized potatoes. Slowly they filled up the burlap sacks— a hundred pounds in each. They did not stop until the ground was hard-frozen. It had been grueling, backbreaking labor, but their cellar now held 30 sacks full, enough food for the winter.

One night during those bitter months, Helene heard a soft knock on the door. She opened it a crack. A neighbor slipped in, wringing her hands.

"Frau Hasel, for God's sake, you have to help me!" she gasped. "There is no one I can trust. Please have pity on me!"

Helene pulled the distraught woman into the living room. Frau Neumann usually kept to herself. All Helene knew was that her husband had been killed in battle several months ago.

"Please calm down. What is the matter?" Helene now inquired.

In whispers the story unfolded. Frau Neumann was connected to the underground movement. She had been hiding Jews until the underground was able to relocate them with trusted families in the country. Right now she was harboring a 13-year-old boy. Someone had tipped her off that the Gestapo, the feared secret police, were going to raid her apartment.

"Frau Hasel, please hide this boy for me," she now pleaded. "No one will suspect you. If you don't help me, we'll both be lost!"

Little did Frau Neumann know that Helene was suspect already because of her stance on Sabbath keeping and her refusal to join the party. Helene thought of her own three young children who would be endangered by this action. But she couldn't send this boy to his death. Quickly, she agreed. In the depth of night, the boy arrived. Waiting by the door, Helene silently opened it and let him in. The children were given strict orders to tell no one of their secret guest.

For several days all remained quiet. Then one afternoon Helene answered the doorbell to three men dressed in long black leather coats—the Gestapo.

"Frau Hasel," they began without preliminaries, "you are under suspicion of hiding a Jew in your apartment. We have a search warrant. You know what will happen to you and your family if we find him." It was a statement, not a question.

"Now we are asking you, 'Are you hiding a Jew?'"

Confused thoughts shot through Helene's mind. *Will God forgive a lie if it can save the boy and us? If I tell the truth, we are all lost. Lord help me!*

Stepping out of the way, she finally stammered, "If you want to, you may search my apartment."

"Frau Hasel," the men asked again, "are you hiding a Jew?"

Again Helene invited them to search the apartment.

A third time they asked, "Tell us, are you hiding a Jew?"

Opening the door wide, Helene motioned to the men. "Feel free to search the apartment."

The men looked at each other. Then without another word, they turned and left.

A few days later, the underground picked the boy up and moved him to safety in the country where he survived the war.

In school, Kurt and Lotte were brainwashed daily about Aryan supremacy and Germany's inevitable victory. Whenever large numbers of Frankfurt men were drafted and transported to the front, the children were assembled in the schoolyard where they had to stand with their right arms raised in the Hitler salute while listening to lengthy political harangues. In time the children developed a strategy to cope with their exhaustion. Upon a prearranged signal, a fight would erupt in a corner of the schoolyard. While the staff's attention was distracted, the entire student body switched arms. The harassed teachers never noticed that the rally was concluded by the children saluting with their left arms.

But of more immediate concern than the brainwashing was the problem of Sabbath keeping. School met six days a week. Traditionally, Adventists had gotten permission to have their children exempt from Sabbath attendance. Now things were different. To keep your children home on Sabbath meant that you were suspected of being Jewish.

After deliberation, the president of the Hessian Seventh-day Adventist Conference recommended to the church members that because of the dangerous political situation they should send their children to school on Sabbath until the war was over. "God will understand our extreme circumstances," he assured his flock.

Helene carefully considered his advice. Already she was suspected of being a Jew. Why aggravate the party officials even more? But then she remembered Papa's parting prayer before he left for the war: "Help us to be faithful to what we believe." She determined to be faithful in Sabbath keeping, and asked God for special strength in the face of this temptation. On Sabbath mornings she and the children quietly left the house to take the tram to church.

Soon she received a letter from the principal asking her to his office.

"Frau Hasel," he said, "the teachers are reporting to me that your children are not attending school on Saturday. Are you Jews?"

"No," said Helene. "We are Aryans. But we are also Seventh-day Adventists."

"Please explain to me what is happening."

"According to the Bible," Helene said, "Saturday is the Sabbath on which we are to worship God. Up to now, my children have always been excused from Saturday attendance. I know this is a big decision for you, but I would like your permission to keep them home on Saturdays."

The principal stared out the window for a time, then sighed and shook his head.

29

"Frau Hasel," he said, "I cannot help you. I admire your principles, but I can't support you. I have been accused by party officials of harboring Jews in my school."

He rose to his feet. "I must insist that your children attend school on Saturday. I assure you that I must and will personally check to see they are there. I have been told that I will lose my job if I don't enforce compliance with Saturday attendance."

Helene knew that he spoke the truth. Only a few years earlier, a Jewish family by the name of Frank, with their young daughters Anne and Margot, had moved into the Hasel's neighborhood and had enrolled Margot in this very same Ludwig Richter Schule. At the time a law had just been enacted entitled Reform of the Civil Service, which decreed that all institutions of the Reich, including schools and universities, were to be "cleansed" of Jews. When Walter Hoesken, Margot's principal, allowed her to remain, both he and Margot's teacher were fired by the Nazis.

Helene thought, *Is it really worth creating such an uproar over two hours of school on Sabbath morning? After all, we still have the rest of the day to keep Sabbath and worship God. Do I have the right to jeopardize this man's job? Is God that particular?*

Then she heard God speaking to her heart: "Whoever is faithful in small matters will be faithful in large ones."

She spoke quietly and respectfully. "I am accountable to God, not to you," she said. "I will not send my children to school on Saturday."

"Very well," the principal replied. "I am not responsible for the consequences. What do you want me to say when I am questioned?"

"Send the party officials and school board members to me. God will fight for me if I am faithful."

Helene went home, gathered the children around her and prayed, "Lord, these are dangerous times for us. Give me wisdom to know how to act. Give me courage to stand for the truth. Protect us from the enemies in our own country."

She paused, holding her children close. "Lord," she whispered fervently, "don't ever let my children become more important to me than You are. Don't let them become my idols."

A few days later, the children brought news. Their principal had been relieved of his responsibilities for another reason—he'd been drafted into the army. A few weeks later Helene read in the paper that he had been killed in action.

Herr Doering, realizing that his harassment had failed to intimidate

Helene, chose other tactics. One day some well-dressed women showed up on her doorstep.

"Frau Hasel," they said, "perhaps you do not know about the many ways the Führer supports the women and children of Germany. We would like to invite you to join the Nazi League of Women. If you do, your rations will be increased and your clothing allowances will be raised. You and your children will be sent to the country on vacations and the government will pay for it—and Kurt and Lotte and Gerd will be able to attend summer camp."

They're telling the truth, Helene thought. *I've seen my Nazi neighbors coming back from their vacations rested and tanned, their children plump and well dressed. Yet I want nothing to do with Hitler's system—because if I accept their benefits, I'll be unable to refuse their demands.*

The women made several visits.

"I am sorry," Helene kept telling them. "I cannot join the League."

Yet they kept trying. One cold early-spring evening Kurt opened the door to the persistent women.

"May we see your mother?" they asked.

"My mother is resting. She has a fever," he said.

"This is very important," they said, so Kurt showed them to her bedroom.

The women politely inquired after Helene's health, and then their faces grew very serious.

"Since Germany is now being attacked by enemy bombers," their spokesperson said, "the Führer has ordered that for safety reasons children should be evacuated to the country."

Helene looked alarmed.

"And the Nazi League of Women has been asked to carry out this order," they continued. "We have the papers all drawn up for you. You just need to sign them."

Helene reached for the papers and began to study them carefully.

"Oh, you don't need to read the fine print," one woman said. "You know how tedious that is! It's just a formality. In summary, it just states that you agree to have your children placed in a lovely retreat in Bavaria where they will receive good food and will be taken care of. Now, if you'll just sign, we won't bother you any longer. We will take care of all the details."

Helene, burning with fever, said, "This sounds crazy to me. Children belong with their mothers."

Despite their protest, she read the document and learned that with her signature she would agree to sign her children over to the government to be placed into concentration camps.

Handing back the papers she said, "I will not sign these!"

Dropping their polite facade, the women stood up angrily. "We will report you," said the spokesperson. "There will be consequences! You will be hearing from us!" When the door closed behind them, Helene fell back into the pillows exhausted.

That night the children noticed that their mother's prayers were more urgent, and chillingly different. "Our Father, I ask for your protection from harm and danger. Please let me never be separated from my children. If we live, let us live together; and if we die, let us die together."

Consequences there were, but in ways neither the women nor Helene could know at the time. After the war, when the Americans arrived, Helene saw these same women driven from their homes by the soldiers, allowed to take nothing with them but their handbags.

CHAPTER 4

IN FRANCE AND POLAND

While Helene was fighting her own battles with the Nazis, Franz and the Pioneers were building bridges 50 miles from the French border. Hitler's plan was to invade France.

The French, of course, had long anticipated something like this. For the past 11 years they had been reinforcing their border areas with a series of forts stretching 87 miles.

This was the famous Maginot Line, the most expensive, most elaborate network of fortifications ever built. The entire network was air-conditioned, and electric trains hundreds of feet below ground transported the half million soldiers stationed there from barrack to gun carriage, from arsenal to canteen to cinema and sun ray rooms. The French thought the Maginot Line was impregnable. But in their complacency they had not taken into account the mighty German air force, the Luftwaffe.

On May 10, 1940, Hitler attacked the Maginot Line with a tremendous number of dive-bombers. The next day, 50 Panzer and infantry divisions broke through. The French army, in shock, offered little resistance. Within five weeks their strength was broken, and the German Wehrmacht had reached Paris and was staging a victory parade down the Champs-Elysees, which Hitler himself attended.

That same May, the Pioneers were ordered to leave Nierstein where they had been stationed for the last nine months. Yet even as they crossed their own pontoon bridge for the last time and boarded a train, they did not know what their destination was.

Curiously, Franz stared out the windows to catch names on station signboards: Scheid, Blittersdorf, Saaralben.

Saaralben.

Now he knew that they were in the Saarland area, very close to the French border. But the train didn't stop there—it finally rolled to a stop in

Saargemuend, 50 miles inside France. Even though they were only a day's journey from home, the men were now in enemy territory and felt a million miles away.

The citizens of Saargemuend had been evacuated.

"Heavenly Father," Franz prayed, "with the local people gone, I now have no way to trade food. You know that I have committed myself to eat only what is clean in Your eyes. Please show me what to do."

In the supper line with Karl Hoffman that evening, Franz noticed a tall thin man doling out the portions.

"Who's that?" he inquired.

"That's the new assistant cook," Karl said. "The regular one got sick and had to be replaced. His name is Willi Fischer. Seems to be a really nice guy."

"He's skinny."

Karl nodded. "He looks like a beanpole. But look at it this way—it makes it harder for bullets to hit him!"

When it was Franz's turn, he refused his ration of cold cuts and took only the bread. Willi glanced at him in mild surprise, but said nothing.

However, day after day, as Franz refused pork and lard, Willi became curious. Finally, while slapping a serving of mashed potatoes onto Franz's plate, Willi whispered, "Stop by and see me later when I am done serving food."

Wondering what Willi could want, Franz went to meet him.

"Hey, soldier," said Willi. "I notice that you don't eat pork. Do you have a health problem?"

"No, I am a Seventh-day Adventist and follow the health laws that God gave us in the Bible."

Willi raised his eyebrows. He stared at Franz for a moment.

"Well," he finally said, "I don't know anything about that. But I don't want you to have to go hungry." He glanced left and right, and lowered his voice. "I'm going to help you out. All you have to do is to arrange to go through line last. And whenever we have pork or lard, I'll give you something else as a substitute if I can."

True to his word, instead of two ounces of butter twice a week, Willi gave Franz four ounces every night. When sausage or cold cuts were served, Franz got a double portion of cheese, or occasionally a can of sardines. Evidently God had chosen Willi to take care of his diet.

The Pioneers were ordered to build bridges across the rivers Blies, Saar, and Moder, as well as many of the smaller tributaries and canals in the area. Courage was high—after spanning the Rhine, these small rivers were child's play.

However, they soon discovered new challenges. As they probed the bottom of the Blies for the best location for the placement of trestles, they were stunned by a deafening roar followed by a fountain of water that shot high into the air. The French soldiers during their hasty retreat had still taken time to plant water mines in the French waterways. Now the Pioneers had to employ minesweepers before any building could commence, and German guards patrolled the riverbanks at night to prevent further trouble.

As part of the occupational forces in France, the Pioneers had to inspect and patrol all dwellings to make sure no French soldiers were hiding out. Looting was forbidden, but when no one was looking, the soldiers filled their pockets with whatever they could carry away.

At night Franz was shocked when he saw the jewelry, watches, and other trinkets the men had stolen. Proudly they compared their loot as they bragged about discovering the homeowners' secret hiding places. Franz felt he had to say something.

"You are upright men at home," he said. "You have wives and children. At home you wouldn't steal. Don't let the war change your values and cause you to become thieves here. What would your families think of you?"

The men turned away shamefacedly and began to undress for bed in the strained silence.

As he himself undressed, Franz felt a small, unfamiliar shape in his pocket. What could it be? He reached into the pocket and drew out a spool of thread.

Where had he picked that up?

Suddenly Franz remembered, and his body turned warm with shame.

That morning he had entered a little gray house. He'd searched the kitchen and bedrooms, and had found nothing—just a moldy half-eaten loaf of bread, bureau drawers pulled open, beds unmade. All signs of a hasty departure.

He had ascended a narrow, creaking staircase and was searching the attic when he discovered a little girl's half-finished dress in a sewing machine. A spool of black thread still stood on the spindle. Thread was scarce in Germany; he knew Helene could make good use of it at home. He slipped it into his pocket and forgot all about it.

Until now.

Franz was guilty of the same sin he had just condemned in others. The Bible reader and carrot eater was also the hypocrite. He fell to his knees, overcome with remorse.

"Oh, God, I've done wrong," he prayed. "I didn't think. I didn't think. Lord, I'm no better than they are. Please forgive me. I'll make it right." He found little rest on his pillow that night.

The next morning Franz searched out the little gray house, climbed to the attic, and slid the spool back on the spindle. He left much lighter than when he came. He knew, of course, that another looter would come along and most likely take the entire sewing machine and the thread along with it. He knew that when the owners finally returned they would find nothing left. But when Franz crept away from that attic the second time, he had left behind all desire for that which was not his. He'd walked away from the black strands of covetousness that bind the soul.

In June 1940 orders came for the Pioneers to transfer to Poland. Military trains emblazoned with the blood-red swastika and bearing the slogan *"Raeder Rollen Fuer den Sieg"*—"Wheels Roll For Victory"—transported them into southeast Poland.

Stationed in the towns of Lublin, Terespol, and Trawniki, the men enjoyed moderate comfort. They couldn't help noticing, though, that the country peasants lived in abject poverty. Their homes were mud huts with straw roofs and no electricity. Water was drawn out of a communal well in typical eastern fashion by lowering a long pole until the container at the end hit water. With a wooden yoke across their shoulders, women carried two buckets of water at a time back to their huts.

Adults and children alike were barefoot. Only on Sundays, for their trip to church, did they take shoes—and even then they tied the laces together and hung them around their necks until they were within 100 yards of the church before putting them on.

In Poland, Hauptmann Brandt decided to make more use of Franz Hasel's expertise in typing, office work, and organizational skills acquired during years of doing literature evangelist and publishing work. So now Franz found himself promoted to Obergefreiter (first company clerk).

With the new assignment came privileges. Like other officers in the German army, he was no longer required to carry the standard military-issue rifle but could select a firearm of his choice. To the envy of his comrades, Franz immediately turned in his rifle in favor of a lightweight revolver, which he inserted in his trouser belt.

Now his work was even more exclusively indoors. In the bitter cold of winter, his office was always warm and comfortable. But the privilege he appreciated the most was that he could arrange his work schedule in such a way that he always had Sabbath off.

The war's second Christmas arrived while the Pioneers were stationed in Krasnystaw. Again trestle tables were set up for the celebration. Each soldier received a raisin-studded Christmas cake and a bottle of wine. This time, however, Franz didn't have to bring his own drink—by his place stood a bottle of grape juice.

However, the military mood wasn't optimistic. Last Yuletide, everyone had been mildly surprised that the war wasn't over. This time there were definite signals that the end was not in sight. Even though Germany and Russia had signed a non-aggression pact, dark rumors seeped through the ranks: Hitler was planning an attack on that country.

And there was all-too-ominous evidence to support this. For one thing, the Pioneers had received strict orders to evacuate all Polish civilians from the towns located on the banks of the river Bug (pronounced "boog"), which formed part of the Poland-Russia border.

Also, the Pioneers were ordered to secretly collect bridge-building materials, and to stockpile them behind the waterfront houses while the unsuspecting Russian soldiers on the other side of the river performed their guard duty. The reasoning was obvious: if Germany declared war on Russia and the Russians blew up the bridges, the Pioneers could immediately rebuild them so the advance could continue.

At three o'clock on the morning of June 22, 1941, the rumors came true. Hitler launched the invasion of Russia along its Polish border. The Russians, lulled into a false security by the German-Russian peace treaty, offered no resistance. Totally surprised by the attack, they didn't even have time to dynamite the bridges.

Yet in spite of this auspicious beginning, Franz had a pre-sentiment that unlike the earlier, easier conquests of the west, this battle would be long and bloody. He recommitted his life to God, and felt reassured that he was in God's care.

"One more thing to do now," Franz said to himself. "I've put it off long enough. Now there's no time to waste."

He hurried into town to the carpenter shop.

"Give me a piece of paper, would you?" he asked the owner. On it he carefully drew a shape, which looked like a bracket used to support a wall shelf. "Could you cut me a piece of wood to that shape? And would you take this soap and chocolate in trade for it?"

The edges of the craftsman's eyes crinkled with delight. "Sure."

As the man began to work, Franz stationed himself by the window and watched the people passing on the sidewalk. He'd planned this moment for a long time, and he couldn't afford to be found out now.

Hurry, hurry, hurry . . . He found himself mentally repeating the words again and again.

"Here you are," said the carpenter finally.

Franz thanked him, and slipped the crudely-made gadget into his inside pocket. After glancing both ways, he left the shop.

Back in his office, he took out his pocketknife and began whittling the angled piece of wood until the corners were rounded. Then he opened a tin of boot polish and blackened it till it gleamed. He opened his desk drawer, buried the device under a pile of papers, and made his way to the company cobbler.

"Walter," he said, "I have the feeling that we will be ordered into Russia soon. I'm finding it a little inconvenient to carry my revolver in my belt. Do you think you could make me a standard-issue holster?"

"No problem, Franz," Walter said. "Come back tomorrow. I'll have it ready for you."

The next day Franz picked up his revolver holster expertly crafted out of black leather. Only one task remained. Late that night, under the cover of darkness, he slipped his military-issue revolver into his holster and made his way to the edge of town where he had noticed a small lake. Once there, he reached into his holster and took out the gun.

At that exact moment he heard German voices—soldiers on guard duty. In all his careful planning he had forgotten about the guards. Beads of sweat ran down his face as he crouched behind some bushes.

His thoughts and his prayers mingled. *Lord, don't let me be caught. Why is it taking them so long to get here? Here they come. Be still, stop breathing. Lord, be with me now. They're stopping. They've spotted me. No, one of them is just lighting a cigarette.*

"Wolfgang," said one of the soldiers. "Did you hear something just now?"

"Ah, it's just a rabbit. Don't be so jumpy, man!"

They passed on. Franz waited a few minutes, then stood up. He took a firm grip on the revolver barrel, and with one mighty swing of his arm threw it far into the pond. The splash sounded deafening.

"Wolfgang. What was that noise?"

"I don't know. It's in the water, I think." The guards came running back, their flashlight beams playing over the ground.

If they find me now, I'm lost.

While Franz was lying flat on his stomach not daring to breathe, the guards walked within an arm's length of him. Wolfgang shouted, "Who goes there?"

They waited in silence for a while. Then the other guard chuckled. "Must have been a fish jumping."

"I don't know," Wolfgang said dubiously. "I thought I saw something move." An eternity later, the men moved on, and finally disappeared in the distance.

Trembling and whispering prayers of gratitude, Franz ran back to camp and into his office. There he took the black-polished "bracket" out of his drawer, thrust it into his holster, and buttoned the flap. This would be the only weapon he carried in the war.

"Lord," he prayed, "this is my way of showing You that I am serious about not wanting to kill anyone. I evidently have some natural marksmanship skills, so I don't trust myself with a weapon. Yet now, with this piece of wood, if I am attacked I will have no way to defend myself. I must trust in You to be my protector. My life is in Your hands."

Uneasily, Franz lay down on his cot. Fear would not let him sleep— not fear of facing a potential enemy, but fear of reprisals.

He remembered sobering news he had heard several days ago. Ludwig Klein, a private in another company, had strolled into the kitchen of his unit carrying a bundle wrapped in burlap.

"What have you got there?" asked the cook.

"A lump of butter."

"A lump! How much?"

"Fifty pounds."

The cook stared at him. "I haven't received any butter rations in months. How could you come up with fifty pounds of butter in a starving country? Don't you know the orders against looting? You're crazy to take a risk like that!"

"Don't worry," Ludwig chuckled. "I didn't steal it. It's all above board. I traded for it."

"Traded what?"

"A pistol."

"*Gott im Himmel!* A weapon?"

"Don't worry about it. The locals are good people. They only shoot at targets on shooting ranges."

But that wasn't the end. The major got wind of it, and Ludwig Klein was summarily executed the same evening. To give a weapon to the enemy was treason against the fatherland and punishable with death. How terrible that a German soldier had to perish by the hands of other Germans! Franz knew that if he were found out, he would meet the same fate. Crying out to God again, he finally fell asleep.

On June 30 the awaited order arrived: The Pioneers were to enter Russia the following day.

CHAPTER 5

IN THE BLACK FOREST

Dear God," Helene prayed fervently, "I'm beginning to feel that it's too dangerous to stay in the city. Any day now I might be arrested for defying the Nazi party. Please provide a safe haven for my children and me."

She remembered that in a remote corner of southern Germany's Black Forest lived a Mrs. Fischer, affectionately known as "Tante Fischer." She was a widow and a faithful Adventist believer.

"Tante Fischer," she quickly wrote, "may I and my children come and stay with you? We will do what we can to help with expenses."

"Of course," Tante Fischer replied in a warm, encouraging letter. "If you can help me meet expenses with 25 marks a month, plus a little extra for firewood, I can provide you a room with two beds. Just bring a crib for Gerd, and some bedding and dishes. I will send Mack, my farmhand, to the station every day until you arrive. He will help you with the baggage."

Helene breathed a sigh of relief. A few quick calculations assured her that the government money she received for child and spousal support while her husband was in the army would be enough to pay the Frankfurt apartment's rent plus the Black Forest expenses. Breathing prayers of gratitude, she packed up a few essential household goods and loaded them, herself, and the children onto the train.

To Kurt, Lotte, and Gerd, the six-hour journey was a rapid and wildly exciting one. They were thrilled to be going to the country, and they waved to pedestrians at railroad crossings and watched the telegraph poles fly by. Despite her nagging sense of worry, even Helene was encouraged. It was early spring, and spring lambs gamboled in the meadows beneath new-budding trees.

"Frau Hasel, is that you?" There at the tiny station was Mack, waiting for them with his ox-wagon. Deftly he loaded their goods, swung the children on top, and invited Helene to share the bench with him.

Soon they left the village behind. The ox now plodded along unpaved country roads.

"Mutti," Kurt asked, "what are those things beside the road?"

"Those are shrines," she said. "The people in this part of Germany are strongly Catholic, and they stop to pray at these little roadside altars."

Intrigued, the children studied them closely as they passed. Many of the shrines had bouquets of fresh flowers in front of them, placed there by the devoted to lend greater weight to their petitions or perhaps to give thanks for a special favor.

"Look," Lotte breathed. "There's an image of Baby Jesus. And there's one of Mary!"

Helene, not wanting to dampen their enthusiasm, said little. But in her heart she prayed that God would grant them His special protection. She knew only too well that the very devotion that made the Catholics so faithful in the observance of their religion also drove them to bitterly persecute non-Catholics. How would her family fare in this region so steeped in prejudice and superstition?

"Up there is Frau Fischer's home." Mack pointed with his whip to a house nestled against the mountainside, and soon the ox cart came to a halt in the yard.

Tante Fischer lived in a typical Black Forest farmhouse. The lower part was whitewashed stucco, while the second floor and the roof were covered with weathered shingles. Ruffled muslin curtains decorated the windows, and red geraniums spilled out of window boxes. The ground floor contained stables for the animals while the second story had living quarters for the family. In the wintertime this arrangement allowed the farmer to take care of the animals without having to go out into the snow. At the same time, the body heat from the animals added to the warmth of the living quarters.

Tante Fischer had already spied them and ran to meet them with open arms.

"Sister Hasel," she greeted Helene, "I am so glad you are here. Don't you worry about a thing. Now you will be safe!"

While Mack began unloading the wagon, Tante Fischer led them up the outside stairs to their bedroom. The room was large and airy with a wonderful view over the meadows to the dark, rolling, fir-covered mountains in the distance. Lotte was to share a bed with mother, Kurt had the other bed, and Gerd would sleep in his crib.

The children were anxious to get outside to explore. Quickly they changed out of their travel clothes and ran down the stairs. They dashed around the side to find there a water trough made from a hollow log with the clear, cold spring water splashing into it, a little like a fountain.

Behind the house were the ancient, black fir trees rustling in the wind. A red squirrel looked down from the branches and chattered at them. Around the other side they discovered the stable with one cow and two goats. Chickens scratched in the dirt, supervised by a majestic rooster with iridescent tail feathers.

"Tante Fischer," Helene said as they gathered around the hand-hewn wooden kitchen table for their supper of bread and milk. "Are people mining around here? It sounds like dynamite exploding."

"That's not dynamite," Tante Fischer said. "Those are blasts from the huge cannon they have set up on the ridge above the village. From there they are attacking the fortifications along the French border. We have already created huge gaps."

So the war is present even in this idyllic forest, Helene thought sadly.

Exhausted from the travel and the excitement, lulled by the splashing of the water-trough fountain and the rustling of the fir trees, they slept like bears in hibernation.

The next day, with a prayer in her heart, Helene set out to enroll Kurt and Lotte in school. In these remote mountain areas, the schoolmaster was the second-most influential person in the village, the first being the priest. In this solidly Catholic region, how could Helene persuade him to excuse her children from Sabbath attendance?

When she arrived at the weather-beaten schoolhouse, the tiny windowpanes sparkled in the afternoon sun. The schoolmaster was a kindly white-haired man with wire-rimmed glasses.

"We have evacuated here from Frankfurt," Helene explained to him. "I would like to enroll my son and daughter in your school."

"Frau Hasel, I will be delighted to have them. Let me add them to the roster. What grades are they in?"

The registration formalities taken care of, Helene breathed a silent prayer and said, "I have a special request. We are Seventh-day Adventists. We worship God on the seventh day, the Sabbath, as the Bible says. I would like to have the children excused from attending school on Saturday."

Startled, the teacher took off his glasses and stared at her in consternation.

"Frau Hasel," he said, "I have never heard of Seventh-day Adventists. I of course respect your religious preference, but there is no way I can allow your request. If I did, it would jeopardize my position."

Helene opened her mouth to reply, but the teacher interrupted.

"Besides," he said, "if the other youngsters get wind of the fact that your children are not coming to school on Saturday, they will want to stay away too. I have a hard enough time motivating these peasant children to come to school in the first place. There is just no way I can help you."

"Please, sir," Helene said respectfully, "it seems to me that it would all depend on how you explained it to the children."

He looked at her thoughtfully for a moment. Then he stood to his feet and ushered her to the door. "I will think it over," he said.

Kurt and Lotte stayed home that first Sabbath and every Sabbath thereafter. Every Monday Helene braced herself for a summons from the mayor—or worse yet, from the priest. But nothing happened. Helene kept praying and wondering.

"Sister Hasel," Tante Fischer said one day at supper, "the mystery of why your children aren't being bothered about the Sabbath is solved."

"What do you mean?"

"This afternoon while I was in town to get groceries, I happened to be walking behind a group of children. I heard their conversation."

Kurt and Lotte glanced up from their bread and milk.

Tante Fischer chuckled. "The boys and girls were telling each other that the schoolmaster had announced that these strangers from the big city were so smart that they did not need to attend school on Saturday!"

Everyone burst out laughing. Again, God had found a way out of the difficulty.

Now that the Sabbath issue was settled, the family relaxed into a regular routine. Except for school hours, most of the day was spent outdoors, where everyone gathered wood and pinecones for burning. They brought home armloads of fresh boughs to bring the scent of the forest into their very bedroom. Hungry for fresh things after their "potato winter," they spent hours in the pastures picking the tender new shoots of dandelions, sorrel, and nettles, which Helene mixed into delicious salads.

As they tumbled in the lush mountain meadows, they heard the murmur of water and discovered tiny brooks criss-crossing the pastures, no wider than a man's hand and completely hidden by the tall grass. Every day was a delight.

On rainy days they played and hid in the stable or hayloft, and swung from a rope Mack had fastened to a beam. Kurt discovered a crack in the wall in a dark corner and hid a length of chain in it. He challenged Gerd and Lotte to find his hiding place. Though they searched diligently, they never did. (Thirty years later Kurt would return to visit Tante Fischer. He found the chain, by then completely rusted, still in its hiding place in the wall.)

When the weather was pleasant, the little family took long hikes through the forest to the tops of the surrounding mountains. By the wayside they picked wild mint and chamomile blossoms, which Helene dried to use for tea in the winter. When summer came, they helped with the hay harvest. Then there were cherries and plums to pick, and later apples and pears. After their deprived diet, this was like paradise.

The children learned to listen for the cuckoo. Legend had it that if you count the calls of the cuckoo, it will tell you how long you are going to live. Eagerly they counted till the cuckoo's call was lost in the distance. They never did get to the end. Gerd, who was not in school yet, got the numbers muddled. Eins, zwei, sieben, tausend, zehn—he gave up!

Every Friday, as a special treat for Sabbath, Helene made the trek into town to buy the children's favorite, Linzer torte, a hazelnut pastry filled with raspberry preserves.

On Sabbath morning the handful of believers gathered in Tante Fischer's living room for a home Sabbath School and prayer service.

One afternoon in late fall Kurt clattered up the stairs calling, "Lotte, Gerd, look what I have!" He held a tiny black kitten one of the peasants had given him. Kurt named him Peter, and soon Peter followed Kurt everywhere and slept on his bed at night. The three children never tired of his antics, and spent hours enticing him to chase after a small pine cone tied to a long string. When Helene churned milk, Peter got to lick some of the cream till his tiny sides were bulging and he collapsed into a corner purring loudly.

Into this idyll the mailman delivered a letter.

"Tante Fischer," said Helene in a low voice so the children would not hear. "Listen to this. It's a letter from the mayor. He has written to all us evacuees in the village and is ordering us to return home immediately."

"What on earth can the man be getting at?" Tante Fischer sputtered.

"I've read and re-read this letter, and I can't understand it."

"There's no rhyme or reason for that order," said Tante Fischer. "None of you have caused any disturbances. And I haven't heard any complaints from other villagers who have housed evacuees."

Helene lowered her voice still further. "We can't leave, Tante Fischer. Gerd is still running the high fever he got yesterday; he can't travel. And I don't think it's God's will that we should have to go back to the city with its persecution and danger."

She gathered her children together. Without telling them what the mayor's letter had said, she led them in a special prayer for God's protection. Then she walked to the mayor's house confident that God would work things out.

To her dismay, he was adamant. "I am sorry, Frau Hasel," he said. "Everyone has to leave. There will be no exceptions."

Returning home heavy-hearted, Helene told the children they would have to help her pack, since they had to go back to Frankfurt the next day. All three youngsters started sobbing as if their little hearts would break.

"What is to become of our little Peter?" Lotte sobbed. "Oh, Mutti, we can't leave him behind!"

Helene thought for a moment. "Let's take him with us."

This small bit of good news dried their tears for the moment, and Kurt and Lotte quickly gathered their belongings. Meanwhile, Tante Fischer hurried out to make arrangements with the milkman to give them a ride to the station the next day. By evening all the family's bundles were ready.

"Tante Fischer, do you have an old farm basket you don't need?" Helene asked.

"Certainly." Tante Fischer hurried to the pantry and returned with one.

Helene took a long scrap of fabric and sewed a collar around the edge of the basket, and then threaded a string through the upper part of the cloth. When she pulled it tight, it drew the cloth together and made a kind of lid for the basket.

"Do you know what this is?" she asked Lotte.

Her daughter had been watching the process with big eyes. "It's a traveling case for our little Peter," she guessed.

The next morning after a quick breakfast, the bedding was tied together. The milkman arrived in his smart wagon drawn by a chestnut mare. He helped them load their belongings, and set Peter's basket right beside his seat.

"Goodbye, Tante Fischer," the children chorused.

"Goodbye," she replied, wiping her eyes on the edge of her apron.

"Thank you for your kindness and generosity to us," Helene said fervently.

"I will pray for you, Sister Hasel. Go in God's care."

As soon as the wagon started, Peter the kitten went berserk in his basket. He screeched. He tore at the cloth in a frenzy. They could hear his little claws clattering against the wicker sides.

Finally the mailman had had enough. "Frau Hasel," he said sternly. "You can't keep that animal cooped up in there. He is frightened. Take him out and hold him in your arms."

Helene followed his advice, and sure enough, Peter settled down immediately and was content to simply look around. At the train station, Helene stuffed him into the front of her coat, where he promptly fell asleep.

The station was crowded with people. The bombing had become very heavy, and train travel was dangerous. Rumor had it that this was the last train out of the Black Forest, and not only were all the evacuees departing, but local people for many miles around wanted to seize this last opportunity to take care of matters in other places. So when the train finally arrived, it was already full.

"Stay right here on the platform," Helene said to the children. "Lotte, watch Gerd. I'll be right back."

Carrying as many of their belongings as she could, Helene climbed onto the train and hurried desperately from car to car looking for space. Spotting an empty corner, she threw down her belongings, then raced back to where the children stood.

"Kurt. Lotte. Up." She pushed them on board, then picked up the still-feverish Gerd and climbed on, just as the train began to move.

As they made their way through the train, Helene noticed that all the compartments were full, and in the aisles there was standing room only. Helene laid Gerd down in their corner and propped his little head against a rough canvas rucksack. He was too sick to care.

The other passengers shot her hostile glances.

"This woman brings all her household goods with her," someone muttered. "It makes it harder for the rest of us."

Just then Peter poked his head out of her coat. Helene cringed, expecting more annoyed comments. Instead, a man standing next to her grinned broadly.

"Look at that," he said. "You have a kitten in there. That cat has it good. If I could rest my head on your bosom, I would be content, too." Embarrassed, Helene turned away while the rest of the passengers burst out laughing. The tension was broken.

An air raid was in progress as the train pulled into Frankfurt. With the moaning sirens sounding in her ears, Helene bundled her children and belongings into Tram 23 for the trip home.

"Why, Lord?" she silently cried out. "Why did we have to leave the safety of the Black Forest? Why did we have to return to bombs and destruction?"

It wasn't until several years later, when she and her two youngest children vacationed in the Black Forest, that she learned what happened after her departure.

"Remember how you had to leave so quickly?" Tante Fischer said. "The very day after you left, the Moroccans invaded our village. They were maniacs, full of rage. They plundered, they destroyed, they set fires. Systematically, they went to each house, found the girls and women, and raped them, from the 5-year-olds to the 70-year-olds. It was all the same to them."

Helene froze in horror. "But what about you?"

"I dressed myself in rags and blackened my face with soot while listening to the screams of the women. The farmer on the hill above me had started a fight with a band of Moroccans to give his two daughters a chance to escape and hide in the woods. Now the men were enraged and tore down the hill shrieking like devils.

"I stepped out of my door with a cudgel in my hand, screaming at the top of my voice and acting like a madwoman. Those superstitious men must have thought I was a witch, for they fled without a backward glance. So I escaped. But for months afterward, the hospital in town was giving free abortions to women and children who had been raped. It's good that you and Lotte were safe."

Now Helene understood. For reasons best known to Him, God had indeed covered her with His wings.

CHAPTER 6

INTO THE UKRAINE

Like France, Russia had been preparing for war. But unlike France, Russia was ready. By the time Hitler launched his attack, the Red Army had become the largest in the world, its warplanes equaling the rest of the world's air forces put together, its tanks outnumbering the rest of the world's tanks.

Yet in spite of this formidable force, the German Wehrmacht was phenomenally successful at the beginning of the Russian campaign. Stalin, reassured by the non-aggression pact with Germany, had left the western border mostly undefended. So when Germany struck, there was little resistance.

Since Hitler's intent was to defeat Russian forces in three to four months, he sent his troops into Russia at a rapid rate. And in the first two days of the offensive, this goal seemed realistic. The Luftwaffe swooped in and destroyed 2,000 Russian planes before they ever had the chance to leave the ground—well nigh eradicating the world's largest air force.

In one week the Germans were halfway to Moscow. In two weeks, half a million Russians had been killed and one million soldiers taken prisoner. In the first month, Hitler's forces had won an area twice the size of their own country. In just two engagements, the Russians lost 6,000 tanks.

At 5:00 a.m. on July 1, 1941, just eight days after the initial assault on Russia, the Pioneers were ordered to cross the Polish border and enter the Ukraine at Sokal. An electric sense of danger filled the air as they stepped onto Soviet soil. Franz felt it keenly.

We're part of the eastern front now, he told himself. *We're no longer just bridge builders like we were in Poland. We're going to have to fight our way forward into new territory.*

Nervously his palm polished the top of the gleaming black holster. Underneath its flap he felt the bulk of his useless wooden pistol. *Lord God of heaven and earth,* he prayed, *please preserve me.*

Day by day, the Pioneers developed new routines. Since enemy activity might explode anywhere, before relaxing after each day's march, they had to carefully search their camping area for Russian soldiers in ambush.

Everywhere they saw signs of active combat. They passed a cemetery where a previous German unit had hastily set up a prisoner-of-war camp, and from which the Russian prisoners stared at the passing Pioneers with hate-filled eyes. Twisted Russian tanks and planes and trucks sprawled across the landscape with fly-covered bodies of the crew lying beside them. A field full of chillingly fresh graves marked the spot where a whole unit of German soldiers had been wiped out by the Russians.

With Friday approaching, something else began to weigh heavily on Franz's mind.

"Dear Lord," he whispered fearfully through dry lips, "You know I treasure Your Sabbath. It's important to You, and because it's important to You, it's important to me. Up to now it's been pretty easy for me to keep Your day by trading work. But now we're at the front, and the rules have changed. Please help me."

And week by week, help came.

"The troops are exhausted," the Hauptmann suddenly announced that first Friday. "We will have a rest day tomorrow."

The next Friday heavy downpours bogged the army down in mud. "We must wait a couple of days until these unpaved roads are dry enough to proceed," declared Hauptmann Brandt.

As the weeks went by, Franz noticed that God arranged events so that his Sabbath hours were protected. All the way to the very end of the war— except for one period of final hectic retreat when he lost track of time— Franz kept every Sabbath.

Farther and farther east the Pioneers pushed. Druzkopol, Berestecko, Katerinovka, Jampol, Belogorodka—unfamiliar names in a strange country. Their motorized vehicles had been sent ahead, so the men were on foot. Yet carrying their guns and field packs, they often covered 30 miles a day. They were chillingly alone—cut off from all communication with other German forces—and their provisions ran so low that finally they had only old bread to eat, green and hairy with mold.

The Pioneers weren't used to prolonged marching, and the exertion finally began to take its toll. As men fell by the wayside suffering from heat stroke, their buddies would carry them over to the shade of a tree, wrap moist handkerchiefs around their heads, and leave them to their fate. The company had to move on.

Some men developed such blisters on their feet that they could not tolerate boots any longer. They'd tug them off and limp along barefoot for a few miles till their bleeding feet could carry them no longer. No amount of pleading by their comrades or upbraiding by their commanders made a difference.

"We're exhausted," they said. "We just can't go on. Please, please leave us and go." The lucky ones became prisoners of war. But most were killed outright by the vengeful Russians.

Franz, too, was exhausted. After a few days his socks were in shreds, and huge blisters soon covered his feet. When the company stopped for a short lunch rest, he looked through his pack to find a clean rag. Everything was filthy, soaked in sweat and covered with the grime of the road.

Finally he took one of his dirty undershirts, tore it into strips and wrapped them around his feet before pulling his boots back on. It was no help. The blisters burst open and became infected. Franz was barely able to drag himself along until 699 made camp for the night. He was running a fever and lay moaning on his mat.

Willi stopped by. "Franz, have you had something to eat?"

"I am not hungry," Franz rasped.

"You must drink something. Come on, sit up." Willi held the tin cup to his friend's cracked lips. "I brought you some boiled water."

Franz choked and coughed, but managed to get down the warm liquid.

"Now eat a bit of bread. You must keep up your strength."

Franz forced himself to swallow a few bites.

Then Willi removed his friend's boots. When he saw the fist-sized festering wounds, he groaned.

"Franz, there is a little stream not too far from here. Lean on me, and I will help you get there. It will give you some relief if you can cool your feet."

With his arm around Willi's shoulder, Franz hobbled the few yards to the water. By the time he reached the creek, his feet had swollen to twice their size. When he stuck his tortured limbs into the murky, polluted water, he did feel relief.

"I can't move," he groaned. "I'm too exhausted."

"OK," said Willi. "Just stay here for awhile. I'll bring your things. All you need is a good rest."

I need more than that, Willi, Franz thought. *My body is worn out and burning with fever. My feet are throbbing with infection. I need days, Willi. Days of rest. But it's not possible. There's nothing more I can do. Tomorrow I'll be left behind like the others. I knew life in the army would be dangerous, but I never thought I would succumb to infection.*

He removed his feet from the water, gingerly dried them. Too worn out to follow his regular routine of Bible reading, he took out his Bible to read just a text before prayer. It fell open to Psalm 118:17: "I will not die but live, and will proclaim what the Lord has done" (NIV).

Stunned, he wrapped himself up in his gray army blanket. Then, lying there on the damp foreign soil, his body shaking with fever, Franz prayed.

"Dear Lord, You know that my life is committed to You. When I left home, I felt assured that You would bring me back safely to my family. Now You have given me another promise. But here I am, sick and unable to continue. Unless You help me, I am lost. I know that You are a promise-keeping God. I commit myself into Your hands."

Finally, Franz dropped off.

Wake-up call at 3:15 a.m. Groggy, Franz rubbed the sleep out of his eyes. His headache and the shaking were gone. *Well, I've had a good rest. If I can get my feet into my boots, maybe I can give it another try.*

He sat up, pulled his feet from under the gray blanket and looked at them. In the dim light they shone whitely.

"Wait a minute," he muttered, blinking and squinting at them. "That can't be."

He reached out his hand and gingerly felt them with his fingers. Then he brushed at them harder and harder.

They're healed. The hair tingled on his scalp. *My feet are completely healed. Not just covered with thick fresh scabs, but with completely new, unbroken skin.*

Shaking his head in wonder, he pulled on his bloody socks, stepped into his boots, and marched stoutly over to wish an astonished Willi a good morning. For the remaining years of the war, Franz never again had trouble with his feet.

The Pioneer Company's trucks rejoined them, and gradually the battalion came back together. Life settled into a routine: wake up between 3:00 and 5:00 a.m. and get on the move. Advance all day, sometimes by truck, often on foot. Spend the short nights in makeshift quarters—barns, churches, synagogues, schools. Usually these were infested with bedbugs that left the men covered with itching, stinging welts. By now, most of the Pioneers also had lice. There was simply no chance to take a thorough bath.

The men were amazed to see firsthand the effect of communism on the country. Decades before, the communists had confiscated all privately-owned land and combined it into huge collective farms, called kolkhozes. Each kolkhoz consisted of fields that stretched from horizon to horizon. The former owners had to work their land like slaves, receiving no pay except the food they needed. The cattle were kept in one enormous barn.

Since working harder wouldn't earn them more profit, the Ukrainians had no incentive to take pride in these farms, and everything was dirty and in poor repair. Only the women were allowed to privately keep chickens, ducks, and geese—and they lavished on them all the attention they neglected to give to government property.

When the hungry Germans came through, they thought nothing of snatching the fowl and roasting them on spits over open fires at night.

"Hasel," they called, "come over and join us!"

"No, comrades, I couldn't enjoy stolen food that you have taken from starving people."

"Well, Mr. Holy Man, don't you know that there is no honor in war? Take what you can get and enjoy it while you are still alive—that's the motto. Besides, Seltenfroehlich took some geese himself. If he can do it, so can we!"

Franz shrugged. "No matter what the lieutenant does, it's still stealing," he said. "And it's still wrong. What if the situation were reversed and Russian soldiers were stealing food from your starving children?"

One of the soldiers spat angrily. "This kind of talk makes me furious," he snapped. "You are so stupid! You know perfectly well that Germany will never be invaded. You always talk as if you didn't believe that. If you don't shut up with your subversive ideas, I'll beat you to a pulp!"

Without a reply Franz turned back to his office. Two days later orders came from the general that all looting was strictly forbidden and that anyone caught with stolen goods would be transferred to a correction battalion where he would be given arduous and dangerous assignments. The stealing stopped.

Franz couldn't help himself. "There you are," he said to the men. "What did I tell you?"

A few weeks after this incident, Franz was promoted again, this time to corporal. He was also made the accountant and paymaster for Pioneer Park Company 699. As such, he kept the books for his unit and handled all the money.

Every 10 days he gave the soldiers their service pay. Because they were part of the eastern front, they were entitled to combat area service compensation. It amounted to one extra Reichsmark—about a dollar every payday. Apparently, the constant peril to their lives was not rated very highly.

Franz also ordered food, clothing, and other provisions from Germany. When they weren't on the march, he set up a small store where the men could buy soap, razors, and other necessities. His superiors did not bother to audit his records—they knew that they could trust him absolutely.

Steadily the company advanced east. Often they passed disabled

Russian tanks; once they passed 2,300 Russian prisoners-of-war marching west to a German prison camp, guarded by only 12 German soldiers. When it rained, the men got soaked to the skin. When there was a cloudburst, the unpaved roads became impassable, and 699 got a day or two of rest. Franz used this opportunity to spread his wet office papers out on the roofs of houses to dry them.

One Friday the sergeant, Erich Neuhaus, came to Franz. "Hasel, I want you to write the 10-day report tomorrow, so I can send it to headquarters."

"Yes, sir." Franz saluted smartly.

"Don't salute me, Hasel. I'm not a commissioned officer. I'm a sergeant."

"Yes, Sergeant. By the way, I want to make you aware that all the paper is wet."

"So?"

"If I put it in the typewriter, it will tear."

"Oh." The sergeant paused. "Well, when do you think it will be dried out?"

"By Sunday."

"All right, do it then."

Another Friday came. "Hasel, you need to do the end-of-the-month close-out of the accounting records tomorrow."

"Yes, sir. But there's just one problem."

"What's that?"

"There's quite a bit of business in the store on Saturday night. Since the first of the month isn't till Sunday, that should really be included in the figures."

"You are right. Better wait till Sunday."

Without seeming insubordinate, Franz always convinced them that the task could be done better if it was done on Sunday.

Sometimes on Sabbath his fellow soldiers approached him. "Franz, can you sell me some soap?"

"I don't know if there's any left. I didn't get any in the last shipment. But if you wait until tonight, I'll do my best to find some for you."

"Oh, of course, this is your Sabbath. I forgot." The soldiers had accepted long ago that they could get no work out of Franz on Sabbath.

In August the rains came more frequently, turning the countryside into a gigantic lake of mud. The Germans, however, were not to be held back. Doggedly they pushed on. When their trucks sank in mud up to the axles, the men heaved them back out. Finally, though, the mud got deep enough to run into the tops of the soldiers' boots, and it took them several hours to travel only a few hundred feet.

"We're so bogged down that we'll have to stop for now," said the officers, shaking their heads. "Even German determination can't defeat the forces of nature."

When the sun finally did come back out, it took the Pioneers an additional two days to tidy themselves and get their equipment back in running order. During the next heavy downpour, they wisely stayed in their billets. Though they didn't know it then, the heavy rains brought the entire war on the eastern front to a standstill. The powerful German Wehrmacht was immobilized—not by the enemy, but by the mud.

Eventually, the Pioneers reached Cherkassy on the western bank of the River Dnepr. Here, where the mighty river was five miles wide, they were ordered to build a bridge across it. They were joined by four other battalions, 6,000 men total, to help them with the formidable task.

Part of the company went to the forests to cut down trees: 21 men operated a Ukrainian sawmill; another 25 a nail factory, which produced not only nails but also braces and metal trestles. The logs were transported to the sawmill, cut into the exact measurements calculated by the engineers, and hauled directly to where the rest of the men were building the bridge.

The Germans ran into increasing opposition from the Red Army, and the advance slowed. Often the battles seesawed back and forth. Squadrons of Russian planes dropped bombs, and German flak cannons shot them down. Then, while the planes lay burning in the fields, the famous German Stukas dive-bombers (short for Sturzkampfflugzeug) swooped in and destroyed the last resistance. Yet no sooner did the Germans relax than the Russians launched a counterattack with tanks—after which the Wehrmacht promptly surrounded the Russians and wiped them out with mortars and howitzers. On and on it went, heavy losses on both sides.

One Saturday the Pioneers were surrounded by Russians. Quickly Lieutenant Gutschalk mobilized them.

"Hasel, you and Weber go into the empty dairy and defend our position on the south!" he yelled.

Here it comes, thought Franz. He cleared his throat and tried to speak calmly. "Lieutenant, today is my Sabbath. I cannot participate."

"What's that, Hasel?"

"I cannot participate. I am sorry, sir."

Gutschalk was stunned. "This is war, soldier! We are fighting for our lives!"

"I am sorry, sir," Franz repeated.

"Hasel, are you refusing an order?"

"Yes, sir," Franz responded, standing at attention.

The lieutenant turned beet red. "I have had enough of you!" he roared. "This time, you will get your just deserts, and nobody will be able to save you! I'll personally see to that!"

After the Russians had successfully been pushed back, the lieutenant made a notation in Franz's Wehrpass (service record) that when the war ended he was to be executed for refusing to obey a superior officer's orders.

The Pioneers, though an engineering unit, were often caught in the fighting zone. One afternoon Franz and Karl did guard duty while the other men were busy fortifying an antitank barrier surrounding a village. Suddenly, there was a flash of fire and an ear-splitting explosion. They ran to the scene and found a soldier named Heinrich Korbmacher with half his face blown off and his bowels torn out—he'd stepped on a landmine. All they could do was hold his head and comfort him while his screams rent the air. "Mother, help me! Oh Mama, I need you! Where are you, Mama?"

Mercifully, his suffering was soon over, and they buried him the same evening. There was not much to say. This loss was especially sad, because the previous spring, Heinrich's little house in Germany had been destroyed by a British bomber.

In death he left a wife and four children behind. As company clerk, Franz had the task of notifying the widow, and of sending Heinrich's few belongings back home to her. Sadly he wondered if someone else would have to perform this duty for him someday.

For the next four years, this was the pattern of life for the German army.

CHAPTER 7

THE BROWN HOUSE

Tram 23, carrying Helene and the children from the train station to their home, clicked and rumbled through Frankfurt's streets as air-raid sirens moaned above.

"Mutti, look." Kurt pointed up at the apartment buildings they passed.

"Where?"

"The windows. All the windows are broken."

Helene's heart sank. "It's the bombs," she said sadly. "When they explode, the air pressure breaks the windows."

"Do you think our windows are broken?" Lotte asked.

"We'll find out soon enough."

Finally the tram ground to a stop. Still half a block away they saw the curtains fluttering in the wind.

"Oh, no," Helene groaned, and thought to herself, *Our apartment is on the ground floor. Nobody has been there to protect it. Everything's probably gone.*

Steeling herself for the inevitable, she led the children off the tram and into the building. As she unlocked the apartment door, the children darted inside.

"It's *dusty,*" she heard Lotte say.

Heart pumping, Helene forced herself to enter. Thick dust and grit covered everything. Her eyes flicked back and forth, up and down.

"Children," she said faintly. "I don't think anything's been taken."

"Here's my castle," Kurt said, "and the tin soldiers."

"And look," said Helene, "the pots and pans, the table linens, and Lotte's doll bed. It's all here. Nobody has touched it."

While Kurt and Lotte excitedly ran from room to room, Helene quickly made up Gerd's bed and tucked him in. He still had a high fever. Then she collected the children, and together they knelt in prayer. "Thank you, God, for Your protection over us—and over our belongings."

Kurt and Lotte unpacked the bundles and put things in their accustomed places. Meanwhile, Helene went to the storage room in the basement and came back with large sheets of cardboard. These she quickly nailed over the open windows.

"It's dark in here," Lotte complained.

"But at least the cold wind isn't blowing in," Helene reminded her. "It will have to do until I can get the glass replaced. Now children," she said firmly, "we've had a long ride, and we're tired. We need to get to bed."

After a few days Gerd recovered, and they fell into their old routine—with one terrifying exception. The children went to school, and Helene did her household chores, but now every night bombs fell on Frankfurt. Daily they prayed that God would protect them and spare their lives. Gerd, who was now 7, was never concerned about their safety.

"The bombs can never hit us," he said confidently.

"How do you know?" Kurt would ask.

"Because we are under the protection of God."

Then the neighboring city of Darmstadt was bombed. In one night thousands of people were killed. Gerd's faith in God's power was still unshaken. He was certain that the church members there had been spared.

In church on Sabbath they were happy to see their old friends and their cousins Anneliese and Herbert. Franz's sister Anni warmly embraced Helene. After church Tante Anni invited them home for lunch.

"Have you heard the news?" she asked gravely.

"News?"

"Most of the Adventists in Darmstadt have been killed. About 80 of our people."

Helene glanced at Gerd. His young face had gone pale, and his eyes stared ahead unseeing. For young Gerd it was a terrible shock. All afternoon—while Kurt and Lotte played happily with their cousins, and Helene and Tante Anni exchanged news of the last several months—Gerd sat quietly in a corner trying to make sense of the Darmstadt disaster.

That night at worship he could hold in his feelings no longer.

"Mutti."

"Yes, Gerd?"

"Mutti," He spat each word from between his trembling lips, "the Bible is all lies!"

"Now, Gerd—"

"God doesn't protect us," he sobbed. "He doesn't care what happens to us. We might as well not pray any more!"

"Gerd. *Gerd*. Listen to me." Helene's voice was soft to match his grief.

"You have learned an important lesson today. Pain and tragedy can come to anybody, good and bad alike. The important thing is to believe that God loves us no matter what happens. As long as we are His children, it doesn't matter if we live or die because in the end, we will live with Him in heaven."

Silently he tried to absorb what she said.

On Monday morning Helene met Herr Doering on the way to the grocery store.

"Ah, I see you are back," he greeted her frostily. "I wonder if you have reconsidered joining the Nazi party?"

"Herr Doering," she replied, "I have no admiration for the party and have no intention of ever joining it. I don't wish to be bothered again! Good morning." With that she turned and left him standing in the street.

"You Jew lover," his voice hissed behind her. "You will live to regret this!"

At the end of the month she discovered what he meant. Franz's army paycheck did not arrive.

She waited a few days, thinking it might have been delayed in the mail. But no check came. With her husband in the army, it was her only means of support. What could she do?

On Sabbath she mentioned her problems in church, and the members took up a collection for her. If she scraped, the money would get them through till the next check would come. As the end of that month arrived, she eagerly ran to the door every time the mailman came. But no check.

Desperate now, Helene took the streetcar to an outlying town where an old friend lived with her grown son in a cunning little gypsy wagon painted yellow with green shutters.

"Sister Geiser," she said, "what should I do? I have no money. The Party is withholding my support payments. We have no food. I am at my wit's end."

"Sister Hasel," she replied firmly, "the first thing we need to do about this is pray and present your need before God. He will show us a way." The two women knelt in the little house on wheels.

When they got up, Sister Geiser said, "Look, I have some money laid by. I will lend it to you, and when your child support comes, you can pay me back."

Helene shook her head. "I can't accept that. What if something happens and you need it?"

"Sister Hasel, we may all be dead tomorrow. Better that your children have something to eat than for me to hoard the money."

With that she went into the wagon's tiny bedroom and returned with her coat and hat. "Let's go to the bank," she said. There she withdrew her entire life savings.

"Sister Geiser," said Helene faintly. "How can I ever thank you for your generosity? This will keep us alive for six months."

Her heart singing, Helene rushed home to buy some food. During the following days she wrote letters to government and welfare agencies explaining her situation and begging to receive her sustenance check. No response. Finally she wrote to her husband in Russia, telling him of the situation and asking for his advice. Anxiously she awaited a reply, not even knowing if Franz was still alive or if the letter would ever reach him.

A few days later she received a letter from the local party office. Opening it, she discovered that it was from the district leader, asking her to pay him a visit.

"Finally they're responding to my letters," she thought. "Now I'll get my money."

Quickly she donned her coat, and walked the few blocks to the building the Nazis occupied.

When she showed the letter to the receptionist, the girl gave her a strange, pitying look, and disappeared into an office. A moment later she came back out.

"Please," she said, pointing at the open door.

Helene stepped in. Behind a desk stacked high with papers, sat a man with the red face and blue nose of a heavy drinker.

"Frau Hasel." He held up a piece of paper. "Do you recognize this?"

Curiously Helene bent closer. "Yes, this is a letter I wrote to my husband a few days ago. How did this come to you?"

He eyed her sourly. "We take the liberty of intercepting and censoring mail written and received by individuals under suspicion. You admit freely that you wrote this?"

"Yes," Helene said.

"Well, I wish to inform you that it is forbidden to write bad news to soldiers fighting at the front. It is forbidden to tell them anything negative about what goes on at home. This undermines their morale and keeps them from giving their best to the Fatherland."

He slapped the letter down on the desk, and moved it out of her reach. "This kind of subversive activity," he growled, "is treason and is punishable with death!"

Helene stared incredulously. "We have received no money for months," she sputtered. "How are we supposed to live? Isn't it my right to write to my own husband and solicit his help?"

"You have committed a crime," he said coldly. "It will be dealt with. You will hear from us." He flipped his hand in a dismissive gesture and raised his voice to the secretary in the next room. "Next, please!"

Helene went home on trembling legs. Again she asked God for help and wisdom. Several weeks passed, but still no money. Doggedly she continued her campaign of telephoning and writing to local agencies for the missing child support. No one responded.

Finally a letter arrived from the Nazi party headquarters in central Frankfurt. It ordered her to appear before Herr Springer, head of the Party in central Germany, on the following Monday morning at 10:00.

Feeling totally boneless, Helene sank onto a chair at the kitchen table and read the letter again. She had heard of Herr Springer. He had the reputation of being the most ruthless and cruel of the local party officials.

And the headquarters! People referred to it as the Brown House because of its brown-stuccoed exterior. At the beginning of the war, the Nazis had taken over the building, and now everyone avoided its ominous presence. "Behind those doors," they whispered to one another, "the Nazis commit unspeakable atrocities. Many Germans who enter that building are never heard of again."

Some had heard rumors that a secret underground passage led from the Brown House to the city's Gestapo headquarters, and that undesirables were taken there and then transported to the dreaded concentration camps. Others knew of people who had been tortured in the Brown House and forced to confess.

And now Helene had to go to this place!

What should she do? Maybe she could take the children and go into hiding. But even in hiding, they would need money for food. On the other hand, if she went to the Brown House and was arrested, what would become of her children?

She fell to her knees. "My Father, I need your help," she cried. "You are my refuge and my fortress. You have promised that you will deliver me from the snare of the fowler. I claim this promise right now. I commit myself and my children under your care."

As she stood up, a calm settled over her.

All she told the children was that she'd have to visit the Brown House on Monday, and that they should pray about it. On Sabbath before the church service began, Helene pulled aside various church members and held whispered consultations with them. Before the service they had a season of prayer, interceding for her and imploring the Lord to keep her safe.

Monday morning came.

"Children," said Helene, "you will not be going to school today. You will stay right here at home. Do not go outside. Do not look out the windows. And be very quiet, so that the Doerings won't know that you are here. Promise me."

Eyes round, they solemnly promised.

Then she took Kurt into the bedroom and closed the door. A few minutes later, he reappeared, looking scared.

"Lotte," said Helene quickly. "It's your turn. Come into the bedroom."

"Kurt," Gerd asked, after they'd disappeared. "Why are you looking so strange? What's going on?"

Kurt pressed his lips together and silently shook his head.

Then it was Gerd's turn. After firmly closing the door, Helene said to him, "Listen very carefully to what I have to say, because I have time to say it only once—and your life may depend upon it. I have to go to the Brown House in a few minutes. You will quietly stay in the apartment all morning. Don't walk around and don't make any noise so the neighbors won't hear you. Do you understand?"

Gerd swallowed and nodded.

"If all goes well, I will be back well before noon. But the Brown House is a dangerous place, and I may not return. I have made arrangements with families in the church to take care of you and the others. If I am not back by 12:00 o'clock, I want you, one by one, to very quietly sneak out of the house. You, Gerd, will go to the tram stop and take tram number 23. At the seventh stop, get off and take number 17 for four stops. Get off, and someone from the church will wait for you there and take you to a secret hiding place. Remember that you will be safe with the church.

"Each one of you has different directions. Do not tell Lotte and Kurt what I have said to you. That way, if the Gestapo find you, you will not be able to give each other away. Now, repeat the directions to me so that I know you got them right."

Gerd was only 7 years old, but he recited the instructions accurately. He understood the seriousness of the situation. Helene knelt with him and prayed for God's watchcare over him and over her. "Always remember, Gerd," she told him, "that God is our heavenly Father, and He will be with you even if something happens to me." She took his hand and led him out.

After donning her coat and hat, she whispered, "I may not see you again. They are not after me, they are after you. They know that they cannot make me change my mind. But if they get hold of you while you are young, they think they can break your mind. Stay true to God whatever happens. Remember not to wait past noon."

With that she quietly closed the front door behind her. Standing well back from the window, the three children peered through the lace curtain and watched her make her way down the sidewalk to the streetcar stop known as Lindenbaum, so-called because of a 400-year-old linden tree growing there.

They quietly settled down with books. They tried hard to read, but found it difficult to concentrate, and often looked up to meet each other's frightened gaze. Fearfully they watched the clock as hour after hour passed.

By 11:45 a.m. their mother was not back.

Standing in the center of the room, they anxiously peered toward the streetcar stop. No sign of mother.

"We have to get dressed," Kurt whispered. They tiptoed into the entry and put on their shoes and coats.

Five minutes to 12:00. They heard the bell of a streetcar as it pulled away from Lindenbaum. One last look out the window. Then they saw a figure running down the sidewalk. All caution thrown to the wind, the three rushed to the door.

"Mutti, Mutti, you are back! What happened?"

Hugging each one, Helene sat down and said, "Now we will thank God because he has performed a miracle." Then she told them about her morning.

She had made her way downtown, arriving at the Brown House a little before 10:00. Glancing up at the menacing façade, she saw barred windows set in foot-thick stone walls. She noticed that there was no doorknob in the steel door. This looked more like a prison than a government building!

Perplexed, she wondered how to enter when she detected a small button set into the wall. She pushed it and heard a distant bell. When a buzzer sounded, she pushed the door open and stepped inside. Behind her the door closed again with a soft click. She turned, and saw that there was no doorknob inside either. Once you were in, only someone with a key could let you out.

A uniformed man peered through a small window.

"May I help you?"

Helene swallowed. "I have an appointment here at 10:00."

"Let me see your summons." He glanced at the letter she'd received. "Oh, yes. With Herr Springer. Third floor, number 11 on the left." The window shut with a bang.

Fearfully Helene climbed the stairs in the ominous, dark house. She met no one, but felt herself surrounded by angels. She knocked on the door.

"Come in!"

Once inside, she approached a dark walnut desk on top of which was a thick folder and a polished brass nameplate engraved with "Gauleiter Springer." The man behind the desk was slender, and had a high forehead, slicked-back brown hair, and narrow-set, small, blue eyes.

He pulled a thick folder toward him.

"Frau Hasel, I have documents here that are very condemning. You refuse to join the Party or the League of Women. Your children don't attend school on Saturday. You have written a subversive letter to your husband. For years you have resisted all our efforts. It sounds very suspicious. Are you a Jew?"

"No, I am Aryan for 10 generations back and have papers to prove it."

"Then what is going on? Why do you refuse to cooperate?"

"Sir, I am a Seventh-day Adventist." As she spoke, Helene suddenly felt light and free. All fear was gone. Boldly she continued, "In the Ten Commandments God asks us to worship Him on the seventh day and to keep that day holy. God's laws are still valid today. That's why I keep the Sabbath."

While she spoke, she studied the man's face, but could read nothing in his stern expression. He picked up the telephone receiver and spoke to his assistant. "Please check if Frau Helene Hasel is a member of the Seventh-day Adventist Church."

Within minutes the phone rang. "Information confirmed."

"Frau Hasel. You have a lot of nerve to speak openly of keeping the Sabbath at this dangerous time—and in this very house!" He paused, studying her for a moment. Finally he said, "It so happens that I am acquainted with Seventh-day Adventists. Do you know the Schneiders?"

Helene knew them well. Brother Schneider was an elder in the church.

"The Schneiders are our neighbors. When we were bombed out and moved next door to them, they invited us for dinner and gave us towels and bedding so we could make a new start. They made a great sacrifice. They are wonderful people. I have a lot of respect for Adventists."

Helene was astonished. The Schneiders had never mentioned that the cruel party boss was their neighbor.

"Now, Frau Hasel," he said, "I want to get to the bottom of this whole situation. You say you have not received your child support payments. What do you think is the reason? Please tell me freely what your suspicions are."

Helene told of the continuing harassment from party members and their hatred for her because she would not join.

"I want you to know that I will never join," she said respectfully but firmly. "I will continue to keep the Sabbath. I am going to be faithful to God no matter what the consequences. I must follow my conscience."

He stood to his feet. "Frau Hasel, I admire your spirit. I am going to check into this. I believe that everyone should be free to believe as they choose. Don't worry about the money. I will see that you get it."

Helene was stunned. Finally she was able to choke out a few words.

"Herr Springer," she said, "I don't know how to thank you for your kindness. May God bless you!"

With a fathomless expression on his face, the man stood up to open the door for her.

"Frau Hasel," he said, "Herr Springer woke up very ill this morning. He was unable to come to work. I am simply filling in for him today."

Helene flew down the stairs with a light heart. Obviously informed about her coming, the man behind the window now awaited her with the key to open the door. He gave her a formal bow as he let her out.

A few days later Helene was notified that she could appear at the child welfare office to pick up a check. It contained all the back payments as well.

CHAPTER 8

WINTER BATTLE

Far to the east, Franz and the Pioneers advanced at a steady pace through Russia into the Ukraine. At first things had gone well for the German Wehrmacht—by August of 1941, the Soviets had lost 3 million men.

In the Ukraine, however, the Germans ran into problems no one had foreseen. Marching day after day through level fields of corn and wheat, they had little by which to measure their progress. As boys, they'd grown up among hills and trees, and they found this flat vastness depressing and disorienting; morale was very low. And with the coming of fall, rains became more frequent, turning roads to quagmires that were impassable to all but tanks.

Nevertheless, the Pioneers continued east. They reached Kremencug, where Company 699 got separated from the rest of the battalion. For a week they were isolated without provisions of any kind, and the hungry soldiers began muttering about mutiny.

One morning Franz went to the huge fields looking for something to eat. All he could see was corn. Corn was not grown in Germany, and he was unaware that humans could eat it.

Gingerly, he broke off an ear and started peeling the husk back. Then he took a tentative bite. The corn was not ripe yet, and the kernels were soft and milky and very sweet. Franz ate his fill. Then he loaded his arms with as many ears as he could carry, and walked quickly back to camp. *I wonder what they'll think,* he asked himself. *They're always making fun of my vegetarianism.*

"I have found something to eat," he announced as he strolled into camp.

Eagerly the men came running. When they saw what he carried, their excitement turned to anger.

"Hasel, you don't expect us to eat that garbage! That's pig food!"

"No, really," said Franz. "It tastes very good."

Two or three soldiers swore, and turned on their heels.

"Look, men. You're starving," Franz implored. "Just give it a try. I'll make a deal with you. If you don't like it, I'll let you spit the kernels in my face!"

Finally a hand reached out and took an ear. Wordlessly, the man bit into it, then quickly ate it all the way to the cob and reached out for another. More than anything Franz could say, this convinced the others. Soon the whole company headed for the field and satisfied their hunger. The vegetarian had saved the day! After a few days, they joined up again with the rest of their company, and the crisis was over.

Now the rains came in earnest, and it became bitterly cold. In Novo-Moskovsk the Pioneers had to stay for a month before the roads were dry enough to continue. When they went on, they covered only 50 miles a day.

Then in October snow fell. It soon became apparent that the German summer uniforms and lightweight boots were woefully inadequate in this inhospitable climate. But on and on they pushed.

"Hasel, come here," said Sergeant Erich Neuhaus one day.

"Yes, Sergeant?"

"I want to see you in my quarters immediately."

Once there, the sergeant said, "Hasel, I notice that you are the only man in our company who has not gotten so much as a scratch or a bruise in this war. The bullets always seem to miss you."

"I hadn't thought of it that way, but you might be right," replied Franz, wondering where this conversation was going.

Sergeant Neuhaus grinned. "From now on, you and I will share the same quarters! You are going to be my guardian angel!"

"Yes, sir! Certainly, sir!" Franz saluted, hand to cap.

Sergeant Neuhaus shook his head at Franz's continuing refusal to use the Hitler salute, but from then on, Franz and Sergeant Erich shared housing. Franz soon discovered that the two of them were often better off than the Hauptmann himself, since the Sergeant had an uncanny knack for discovering comfortable hideouts. It was an arrangement that the two kept for the rest of the war. Even the nicest quarters, however, were cold, dirty and infested with fleas and lice.

On a kolkhoz one night, the whole company decided to bed down in a gigantic barn warmed by the bodies of hundreds of cows. As they gathered bundles of straw for their beds, they noticed that the place was overrun with rats. In disgust the men pulled themselves up onto the rafters and laid boards across the beams to provide sleeping platforms. They placed their bread bags, which contained all their food, securely under their heads for protection, and went to sleep high above the vermin infested floor.

Next morning they discovered that the rats had scuttled along the rafter beams, gnawed holes into the bags, and eaten the food from under their very heads. Not a crumb was left. Furious, the men hunted for the rat holes outside the building. Arming themselves with sturdy sticks, they took their positions. Whenever they saw a whiskered rat-face peering out, they struck with all their might. In this manner they killed 30 rats in 10 minutes. They were avenged—and could now move on.

Only once in all their journeying did they see a beautiful village. Checking the map, they learned it was Huttich. The houses, while built of mud in the Russian rural fashion, were covered with white stucco that shone in the sun. The streets were clean and free of trash. The mud floors were swept, and the windows had crisp curtains made of colorful cotton prints. What a joy it was to spend even one single night in a place that looked like home!

The next goal was Kramatorsk to the south. The temperature dropped steadily. There were no forests in this farmland, so the soldiers tore down fences and decrepit buildings along their route and carried the wood with them so that they could have fires in their quarters at night.

"You'll be staying here for some time," they were told. "You will need to repair a sawmill, because several bridges need to be built across the Donetz River." Soon the Pioneers were busy doing some of the work they'd been trained for—cutting wood and preparing steel trusses.

Thus another Christmas arrived. How different it was from the rowdy celebrations of previous years. On Christmas Eve the Hauptmann conducted a somber church service remembering the many comrades who had already lost their lives.

Afterward there were no festive tables set with spice cakes and wine. Instead a different surprise awaited the soldiers. In the afternoon 12 sacks of mail had arrived. Now, as each soldier received longed-for messages from home, there was greater happiness in the unit than had ever been at the noisy, drunken parties of previous holidays. It was the best Christmas present for the men. Quietly they returned to their billets to read their letters and mentally spend Christmas Eve with loved ones at home.

Franz discovered that a letter from his mother had taken 85 days to reach him, and one from Helene had taken more than three months. He himself had written a Christmas letter to his family weeks before. He got a comrade to decorate it for him with a drawing of the stable in Bethlehem, complete with a cow, a donkey, and some sheep. Above them sparkled a bright golden star. He wondered if they had received it.

New Year's Eve was also different. They huddled together in the community hall and talked. For most of the men it was the first time in their lives that they welcomed the New Year without a drop of alcohol. Soon the conversation turned to politics and their hopes for the future.

Suddenly Lieutenant Gutschalk said, "The Führer is my god! My trust rests in him!"

"Sir," Franz exclaimed without thinking, "You have a sorry god!"

Face red, Peter Gutschalk jumped up. "What? You dare to take the liberty to say something like that?"

Franz realized that he had blundered. Hastily he tried to make amends.

"Yes I did say that," he said, "and I'll say it again. But what I meant was that Hitler is human like you and me. And one day he will die like you and me. And when he is dead, you won't have a god any more. Isn't that sad?"

Then Franz pointed to a piece of bread on the table. "See this bread, Peter? Hitler didn't make the wheat it grew from—only our Creator God can do that."

His chin quivering with rage, the Lieutenant roared, "Hasel, you have gone too far this time! I will see to it that there are repercussions!"

Suddenly the Hauptmann jumped to his feet. With a voice cutting like steel, he said into the silence, "Men this is New Year's Eve. We're having a private conversation. There will be no repercussions! Good night!" With that he turned on his heel and went out.

The mood had been broken, and the others also went to their quarters. Franz realized that he had said too much this night. In his room he took his Bible and reread Amos 5:13: "Therefore the prudent shall keep silence in that time; for it is an evil time" (RSV). He determined to be more careful in the future.

On the surface things settled down again, but when a few days later Franz passed Gutschalk and saw pure hatred in his eyes, he knew that the insult had not been forgotten.

In January there were daily skirmishes with the Soviet troops. During one gun battle a Pioneer seemed to be lightly wounded. By the time the men could carry him to safety, he was dead. In shocked silence they examined him and discovered that in addition to the shot that grazed his thigh, another bullet had gone to his heart at the same time. The same afternoon they dug a grave for their comrade and then assembled for the short service the Hauptmann conducted. Within 10 minutes in the bone-chilling cold, the Hauptmann's ears were frozen. The temperature was minus 35° F.

Back at home Reichsleiter Goebbels, unable to procure warm uniforms for the Wehrmacht, had launched a campaign to collect winter clothing and women's furs from the German people. The donations, however, were woefully inadequate, and none of them ever reached the Pioneers.

Resourceful as always, Franz spent the evening after the funeral figuring out how he could protect himself from the cold. He took two socks, cut the feet off, and laid them aside. Then he cut each of the long parts open and stitched them together. Finally, he gathered one end of the wide tube and sewed it together. Now he had a makeshift cap that fit over his ears.

In the morning, when he emerged from his billet, the others pointed and laughed.

"Vegetarian, what crazy idea have you come up with now? You look like a scarecrow! You are a disgrace to the German Wehrmacht!"

Unperturbed, Franz grinned. "You just go ahead and laugh. At least my ears are warm!"

In the course of the day, the temperature dropped to −45° F. Twenty more men froze their ears. The next morning every member of Company 699 wore a cap made out of socks.

Franz was fortunate that he had an office job. Even though the ice on the windowpanes of his office was sometimes two inches thick, as long as he was indoors he could keep warm. And when he had errands to run outside, he bundled up. He pulled on three pairs of pants, two coats, and two pairs of gloves. On his head he wore two scarecrow caps and topped them with his regulation army hat. Finally, he wrapped a scarf around his face so that only his eyes were free. Then he ventured out.

When the company had to assemble outside, noses were frozen within three to four minutes. The Germans, unused to such conditions, tried the most logical remedy. They took the men suffering from frostbite indoors and set them next to the hot stove. The rapid warming created greater damage.

"No," said the Ukrainians who saw what was happening. "You must first rub the frozen part with snow until it gets glowing hot and tingles. Then you know that circulation has been restored and the part has been saved."

Even so, the Pioneers and the rest of the German army suffered heavy losses due to the cold—fingers, ears, noses. Often feet and legs had to be amputated. During the coldest part of the winter, within a period of just two weeks, fully one-quarter of the Wehrmacht stationed in the Soviet Union was disabled because of frostbite damage. The brutal temperatures, sometimes dipping to −60° F, lasted for many weeks.

But while the Germans were almost paralyzed by the cold, it seemed to effect the Red Army very little. Through the month of January, the Pioneers were on the receiving end of daily bombings and artillery attacks. Each time there were casualties, soldiers as well as civilians. German planes supplied the Pioneers with ammunition and food, and flew out the sick and wounded.

While they were staying in a basin in the Donetz area, the planes stopped coming, and Company 699 was cut off from supply lines for a couple of weeks. They had just come through a heavy battle that left them with only one functioning tank—and not a single round of ammunition.

Surrounded by Russian forces, they resorted to trickery to fool the enemy. They drove the tank up the hillside on the right, steered it along the crest for a little while, then quickly down the valley, changed license plates, up the left side, down, back, front, left again. Twenty-four hours a day they kept it up. Fortunately the many Ukrainian oil wells kept them well supplied with diesel fuel, and the single tank seemed omnipresent. The Russians, intimidated by this display of military prowess, dared not attack, and eventually airlifted goods came through again.

As January turned to February, then March, the temperature slowly warmed, sometimes reaching 0° F. Like hibernating animals, the Wehrmacht emerged from their billets where they had holed up for the coldest months. The German advance started up again.

Unlike the previous summer and fall, however, the Red Army fiercely fought back. The Germans could no longer parade confidently along, but had to inch their way forward under heavy artillery fire. The Pioneers built a bridge over the river Torez, this one made entirely of steel pipes welded together, and continued eastward. Later that spring all survivors of the winter battle were awarded a medal. However, no compensation could make up for the hardships they had endured.

In a large village one evening, another unit caught up with them and shared their quarters. The tall men in their distinctive black tailored tunics with silver skull-and-crossbones insignia on their visored field caps belonged to the Schutzstaffel (the SS), Hitler's elite military and police corps. On their arms were blood red armbands with the black swastika in a white circle. Known for their cruelty and their unquestioning loyalty to Hitler, they inspired fear even back in Germany.

Late at night Franz was torn from sleep by a commotion in the village. Running, banging, the crack of splintering wood doors, German voices cursing, the screams of women and children. Finally, it became quiet. He thought he heard gunshots in the distance, but he was not sure.

At the end of the food queue the next morning, Franz sought information from Willi Fischer. "Willi, did you hear that noise last night? What was going on?"

Willi glanced furtively around. "That was the SS," he whispered, "doing their duty."

"Doing their duty? What do you mean?"

Willi's voice dropped even further. "Hitler's final solution!"

Franz looked at him uncomprehendingly. "I don't understand you."

"Where have you been, man? They are liquidating the Jews. They round them up, take them into the forest, and shoot them like animals."

Stunned, Franz simply stared at Willi. "Impossible."

"Franz. Just move along, and whatever you do, don't talk about it."

Franz picked up his tin plate.

"I know how you feel," Willi said. "I am not supportive of Hitler either. But we are not responsible for what the SS does. We have our duties, and they have theirs. It's on their conscience, not on ours. If you want to save your own neck, Franz, stay out of it. Don't interfere!"

"Willi, I just can't stand by and—"

Willi leaned over the deck until his face was within a few inches of Franz's. "I know how you are," he hissed furiously. "You are going to open your big mouth and get yourself court-martialed!"

Franz went back to his quarters deeply troubled by what he had learned. He could not agree with Willi that they had no responsibility in this. If they stood by while murder happened, were they not also guilty of murder? As was his custom, Franz took this dilemma to the Lord.

"Heavenly Father," he prayed, "please show me how to relate to this situation. What would you have me do?"

Next day, by the time the Pioneers moved on, he had his answer. He understood now why he had not been assigned to the medics. God evidently wanted him to get to the Jews before the SS did.

From that time on, whenever his company passed through a village, Franz slipped away and stepped into stores, businesses, and as many houses as he could reach. Since the Ukraine was mostly populated by former Germans who'd accepted Catherine the Great's offer to emigrate to Russia and cultivate the land, he could communicate with them easily.

He repeated the same message everywhere:

"The SS is following a day or two behind us. You will recognize them by their black uniforms with skull-and-crossbones on their caps. When they get here, they will round the Jews up like cattle and murder them. If you are Jewish, take some food and your families and leave right now. Hide in the forest or in caves—wherever you can find a crack. Go quickly—there is no time to lose. Spread the word! Just hurry, *hurry!* And may God go with you!"

Many saved their lives because they heeded his warning and disappeared into the countryside. Most of them, however, were more concerned with protecting their property. Holding on to their belongings, they lost their lives.

Franz's mysterious village visits hadn't escaped the eyes of his comrades.

"What business does Hasel have fraternizing with the civilians all the time?" they asked suspiciously.

No one knew for sure; only Willi and Karl suspected the truth. They loyally came to the defense of their friend.

"Leave the guy alone, won't you?" they said. "You ought to be glad he scouts around and buys local goods. Why else do you think his company store is always so well stocked? If he didn't work so hard for you, you wouldn't be able to get fresh eggs and candy and other luxuries."

This effectively silenced the men.

A few weeks later the battle forced the Pioneers to return to a village they'd left the day before. In the woods Franz heard German voices shouting and swearing. His curiosity was aroused. Hiding behind trees, he followed the voices. Soon he came to a clearing honeycombed by trenches Russian soldiers had dug.

The SS men were driving Jewish civilians through the woods. Men, women and children—several dozen of them. Horrified, Franz realized that these were the Jews who had not heeded his warning the day before. Silent and barefoot they walked across the snow.

When they reached the clearing, the soldiers ordered them to kneel facing the trenches. Then, row after row, they shot them in the back of the neck and let their bodies tumble into the trenches. Last of all came a mother with her six children. Sobbing, the terrified children clung to their mother.

"Let go of her!" the SS men shouted. Brutally they tore them away, forced them to kneel and shot them in the neck.

Franz had seen enough. Stepping out of the trees, he approached the men.

"How can you do such a thing and shoot these innocent children?"

The SS men glared at him.

"Man, where have you been all your life?" one snapped. "It's the children who especially have to be killed! If they live to grow up, they will become our greatest enemies. Here!" He grabbed a shovel. "Since you feel so sorry for them, you can at least give them a decent burial. Here, cover them up!"

He tossed the shovel at Franz. The others laughed raucously. Still chortling, they jogged away.

Franz felt ill. He had to lean against a tree for a while to regain his composure. Finally he walked over to the trenches and sadly began covering the bodies with dirt.

Suddenly he stopped. He thought he had heard a moan coming from one of the holes. Yes, there it was again. He dropped the shovel and peered at the bodies. They were still. Then he noticed a small movement beneath one of the children who had been shot with their mother. He jumped into the trench and gently picked up the bloody body of a little girl. She was dead, after all, and he carefully laid her to one side.

But underneath her a man was still alive. Mustering all his strength, Franz picked him up and heaved him out of the trench. The man was unconscious but still breathing. A bullet had passed through his head. He didn't seem to have bled much. Maybe he could be saved. Franz hoisted the man onto his back and headed to the village. His plan was to get him quietly to his quarters and bandage him there.

As he neared the camp, staggering under his load, he was accosted by an SS man.

"What are you carrying there?"

"This man is seriously hurt and needs immediate medical attention!"

The SS man noticed that this was not one of the German soldiers.

"What in—?" he screamed. "We are killing Jews, not saving them! How dare you interfere!"

By now other Pioneers had come running out, among them Lieutenant Peter Gutschalk. One glance, and he understood exactly what had happened. He tore the man off Franz's back. As the man hit the ground, the Lieutenant put his gun in the man's mouth and pulled the trigger.

"Hasel, it's you again!" he snarled, trembling with rage. "I should have known! I am telling you once and for all that I have had enough of your subversive behavior. It's my goal to see you destroyed. You are no better than the Jewish swine you tried to save! You will not escape me. If I have to, I will search the earth over for you. There is no room in the new world we are building for people like you! And that goes for your two friends also!"

Open enmity had been declared. Franz wondered if he would lose his life in the war not by the hand of the enemy, but by one of his own countrymen.

CHAPTER 9

SUSI'S BIRTH

"Give us this day," murmured Helene, "our daily bread."

It was a prayer she prayed often these days. Although she was again receiving her regular government child support allowance, food was harder and harder to find.

Even worse, Helene had been ailing for a while. She didn't have a lot of confidence in doctors, so she avoided them as long as possible. Finally, when she found it hard even to get on her feet, she went to see Dr. Richels.

After a careful examination, he said, "Frau Hasel, you are pregnant."

Helene's mouth fell open. When she could collect her wits, she protested, "I am not pregnant."

"You are pregnant," he insisted. "I will write you a verification that will qualify you for extra rations of bread, rice, milk, and butter."

"Doctor, I know I am not pregnant. My husband is in Russia. He has not been on furlough in months."

Dr. Richels' voice was kindly. "Don't distress yourself, Frau Hasel. I see pregnant women all the time whose husbands are not home. It's just human nature—people get lonely. In the meantime, here is the certificate that will get you extra ration cards. Come back in a month."

Helene left his office shaking her head. But the extra food was a godsend for the children, and supplemented their small garden plot.

Before the war, she and Papa had leased this plot, and now she worked in it daily, using every inch of ground to grow vegetables, which helped them make it through the summer. What they couldn't eat, she canned for the winter. And in the fall, they again went to collect the potatoes left in the fields by the farmers after the harvest. They also took the streetcar to its terminal stop and hiked into the woods where the ground was covered with beechnuts. They filled buckets and buckets with them, and back home, Helene crushed the tiny nuts and extracted a few cups of precious oil.

"How's the baby doing?" Dr. Richels would ask her, month after month.

"I am not pregnant," she would insist.

He would chuckle kindly—and renew her extra rations.

Finally, at seven months, he admitted that he had made a misdiagnosis. This, of course, didn't do much for Helene's confidence in doctors. However, she recognized that God had used this man to provide for her family.

Meanwhile the bombing of Frankfurt continued. Night after night, Helene and the children were torn from sleep by the screaming air-raid sirens. Night after night they hurried through the fearful streets to the bunker.

One night the attack was especially terrible.

"Kurt! Lotte! Gerd!" Helene screamed. "Get up, get up!"

But she couldn't rouse the sleep-deprived children for several minutes, and by the time they reached the street, it was deserted. All around they heard the thin whistle of falling bombs, and then the thunderous explosions.

We're not going to make it to our bunker, Helene thought to herself.

In desperation, she huddled the children toward the basement shelter of a house on the way. Clawing at the door, she jerked it open. Hands reached out, pulled them in, and slammed the door.

In the dim light of a kerosene lantern, Helene made out huddled shapes. She saw that the owners had obeyed government regulations and equipped the shelter with gas masks, buckets of water, and blankets to put out flames. Lined up against another wall were buckets of sand. One of the Allies' dreaded weapons was the phosphorus bomb. When a drop of phosphorus hit your hand, it would burn a hole right through. Water wouldn't stop the burning; only putting your hand in sand extinguished the phosphorus.

As the hits got closer and closer, the basement floor heaved. As they had been drilled, the silent people in the shelter lay flat on their stomachs, put their fingers into their ears so their eardrums would not rupture from the concussion, and opened their mouths so their lungs would not burst from the air pressure.

Finally the bombing began to subside. The group in the shelter was running out of oxygen. Cautiously someone opened the door a crack—to reveal a wall of fire just outside.

Everybody seemed too shell-shocked to do anything. In desperation, Helene took command.

"We must get out," she said, "or we will suffocate." She grabbed the blankets, dipped them into the buckets of water, and handed one to each person. Tightly wrapped, the people dove through the flames. Kurt ran first, then Lotte and Gerd, while she followed last. Gerd, curious to see what was going on, peeked out of his blanket. A flame licked at his face, and by the time they arrived at the other side of the street, his eyebrows had been singed off.

Trembling and bone-weary, they dragged themselves to their apartment. Miraculously, it was unharmed.

The family had received no word from Franz in months. Was he still alive? Only occasionally would the news reveal where the Pioneers were. On a map of Eastern Europe, Helene and the children plotted his course as best they could.

One bleak evening at the end of January, there was a knock on the door. Gerd ran to open it.

"Guten Tag," he said politely to a tall, muddy stranger. Then his eyes widened. "Papa-a-a-a-a!"

Sure enough, Franz was home. He'd been given three weeks' furlough. Hitching rides on army trains and trucks, it had taken him one of those weeks to get home. But now he was here, and he was alive.

The family spent many evenings recalling the dangers they had been through and recounting God's wonderful protection. In the daytime Franz trekked across the city, seeking out coal merchants who could supplement the meager supply of fuel that Helene had left. She, in turn, used her carefully hoarded sugar rations in a cake made of oatmeal, cream of wheat, a little flour, and some baking powder. She had no eggs and no oil. Though the cake was heavy and coarse, the family feasted on the delicacy and enjoyed it more than the feather-light cream puffs they had liked before the war.

With gleaming eyes Gerd inspected the medals Franz had brought back. He secretly took them to school one morning and showed them off to his friends. "My papa is a great soldier," he bragged. "He is helping Germany win the war." Proudly he strolled to the next group of children.

Helene found the medals in Gerd's pants pockets after he had changed into his play clothes. That evening Franz gathered the family around him. He said, "I want you to imagine a country like no other on earth. The people are prosperous and live in nice houses. They have cars and wonderful food every day. The country has many laws. One of the laws proclaims that it is forbidden to worship God. Another law says that the government will kill children and grown-ups who are different. Only the people who are strong, healthy, and intelligent and who follow all the laws of the government will be allowed to live."

The children had been following this fantastic scenario with wide-open eyes. Now Franz asked them, "How would you like to live in a country like that?"

Their answers tumbled out. "It would be horrible! If they didn't like us, they might kill us!" Gerd summed it up best. "I wouldn't be able to enjoy any of the wonderful things because I would be too afraid to leave the house. I couldn't even go to school, in case the teacher thought I wasn't smart enough!"

Franz paused for a long while. Finally he said, "Children, if Germany wins the war, it will become the country I have described."

Much sobered, they knelt for prayer. "Dear Lord, please don't allow us to win the war. Let Germany lose soon so that the suffering will be over."

All too soon it was time for good-byes. This parting was even harder than the first had been because now they realized more than ever that they might not see each other again.

After Franz left, Helene again felt ill and soon realized that this time she really was pregnant. With a heavy heart she went back to Dr. Richels. How, with no end to the war in sight, would she be able to care for a fourth child? Dr. Richels confirmed the pregnancy and again issued extra rations. At least they would make it through another summer.

As the war escalated, the Allies stepped up their bombings of Germany. Every night now the air raid warnings sounded as squadrons of bombers droned overhead. Day after day, as Helene got the mail, she anxiously scanned the envelopes. She breathed a prayer of thanks each time there was not a black-rimmed one among them. She knew the dreaded news they contained. "We regret . . ." they began, and continued, "Your husband has died a hero's death for the Fatherland." Thousands of German women were receiving such letters. Each edition of the newspaper, the *Frankfurter Generalanzeiger,* contained long black-bordered columns filled with names of local soldiers killed in action.

Now the fifth winter of the war was upon them, and a baby about to be born. For the other three births, Helene had been hospitalized. But this one was going to be different. Much of downtown Frankfurt lay in smoldering ruins. The hospitals that still functioned only accepted emergency cases. Aided only by a midwife, women had to give birth at home.

On a freezing, drizzly night at the end of September Helene rested on the couch in the tiny kitchen while Lotte and Gerd washed the dishes and tidied up. It was chilly—the coal rations they had received for the winter were only enough to heat this one room, and the radiator was turned off unless absolutely necessary.

Kurt systematically went from window to window making sure that the blackout curtains were tightly in place. He understood that even a chink of light might give away the location of the apartment buildings to low-flying enemy airplanes looking for targets. Carelessness could cause the death of many people.

All afternoon Helene had been in the early stages of labor. The children seemed to realize how helpless and despondent she was feeling.

"Mutti," Lotte said comfortingly. "Don't be afraid."

"We're going to take care of you," said Gerd. "We will help with the baby."

Helene smiled through her pain. The contractions were now coming at regular intervals.

"Lotte. Gerd." Her voice sounded weak. "It's time for you to go to bed." While the two children went obediently to their room, she turned her head to face Kurt.

"Kurt, dress up well. Put your scarf and mittens on and go out to get Frau Gabel, the midwife."

Kurt stumbled out into the biting night. Blackout rules meant no streetlights, and not a glimmer of light shone from any of the dwellings. The only illumination was an orange glow in the sky, from the fires that were consuming Frankfurt.

As he hurried along, he heard the familiar drone of airplanes and the whistling bombs, then the roar of explosions. The shock of the blasts shook the houses and rattled the windowpanes, and cold air rushed by his ears and took his breath away. Finally, he reached the house of Frau Gabel who grabbed her black bag and followed him into the night.

Back at the apartment, she began issuing orders to him.

"Get lots of water boiling," she said. "Then get some clean sheets and bring them to your mother's room. And it's too cold in here."

"I turned the radiator on not too long ago."

"Fine," she said. "Now you stay out here in the kitchen. I'll let you know if I need you."

Hours later, Kurt heard a tiny wail.

Like magic, Lotte and Gerd appeared in their room doorway, their blankets wrapped around them.

"We couldn't go to sleep," said Gerd. "Is it born?"

The three tiptoed to the bedroom. Lotte opened the door a crack, peeked in, and then opened the door wide.

"Oh Mutti," she exclaimed," the baby is here. Did it hurt much? Is it a brother or a sister?"

Helene smiled weakly and pointed to the cradle where the baby lay already dressed and diapered. "You have a little sister. Her name is Susi."

Delighted, they stood around the cradle and admired the cute little face and the tiny fingers that already had fingernails. They had a little sister! They knelt down by Helene's bed, and together they thanked God for the safe birth and a healthy baby.

"I'm going home," Frau Gabel finally said. "You shouldn't need me any more. Try and get some rest."

The children crept back to their beds and fell asleep. But at four o'clock air raid warnings ripped them from their slumber. Enemy airplanes were overhead again, and no one knew where they might drop their lethal loads of bombs.

Kurt staggered blearily into Helene's bedroom. "Mutti, what should we do?"

"Get the children up," Helene said. "We need to get to the bomb shelter."

"Can you make it? Or should I take Lotte and Gerd while you stay here?"

"No, we must stay together. We will all go. I will be all right."

Quickly they dressed, wrapped the baby in blankets, and hurried out into the icy night. Dark figures streamed toward the bunker half a mile away. Just as Helene stepped inside, the bombing started in the distance. Someone slammed and bolted the shelter's airtight doors.

Almost immediately the electricity went off, and the air circulation stopped. Silently and in total darkness the people waited. There was standing room only.

"Excuse me," whispered Helene, "but I just gave birth only three hours ago."

"Here," someone said, "move over here so you can lean against the wall. Make room for this woman, please!"

Not that it was strictly necessary to lean against anything. The bunker, built to hold 2,000 people, often was jammed with 6,000. Long ago, Gerd had learned that all he had to do was pull up his feet and he was suspended between the packed bodies. Sometimes he even fell asleep in that upright position, legs dangling. More often, though, he had to fight for breath, and it was in that dark bunker that he developed the beginnings of a lifelong claustrophobia.

The shelter began to rock from the pressure of explosions as the bombs dropped closer and closer. Helene felt ill as the air became hot and foul.

My baby, my Susi. . . . She'll suffocate from the crush of bodies.

Protectively she held the tiny head against her chest. Lotte started crying. A priest murmured the Lord's Prayer. Women fainted, but there was no space to lay them down, and they remained upright by the press of the many other bodies.

An eternity later, the all-clear sirens sounded. Someone opened the heavy steel doors, and the cold, fresh air rushed in. Bathed in sweat from the oppressive heat, the people stepped out into the freezing night.

When Helene and the children got back home, all were close to collapse. Helene looked at her exhausted, disheveled children and made a decision.

"Never again will we seek shelter in the bunker," she declared. "From now on we will go to the basement." The apartment building's basement had been reinforced, and it was good for all but a direct bomb hit. *If God wants us to survive,* she said to herself, *He can save us here as well as in the bunker.*

Several times each night air raid warnings sounded, and Helene had to drag the children out of bed and down the stairs. Yet even these trips downstairs became too wearying. Yearning for uninterrupted sleep, she finally set up their beds in the inhospitable basement, and the five of them slept down there.

When Susi was just three weeks old, an order arrived that all women with children had to leave the city. Dismayed, Helene sought Sister Geiser's advice.

"Who in the country will take a woman with four children?" she wailed.

"Don't you worry," Sister Geiser comforted her. "I will go with you and make sure you get settled in." Gratefully, Helene embraced her friend.

At four in the morning, they bundled the children up and headed for the small local station to catch a train to the main terminal in Frankfurt. When the train arrived, it was already packed. Sister Geiser and the three older children were able to squeeze into the first car. But Helene with the baby buggy desperately ran down the length of the train finding no room. At the last minute, a soldier lifted the buggy into a car and hoisted Helene up after it.

Pandemonium reigned at the main terminal. Hundreds of women with their children milled around while League of Women officials tried to direct them to the right trains. Helene was sent to a train traveling to Eschenrod, a small village in the Vogelsberg mountains. There, as well as elsewhere, each farmer had been ordered to house evacuees from the city.

For five hours the families waited at the train station. When they asked about the delay, harried conductors told them that no trains could run because the tracks were under heavy air attack. Helene felt faint and had to sit down on the baggage. The children, though ready to drop themselves, took turns pushing the buggy back and forth to rock the baby to sleep.

Finally the train arrived, and the barriers were opened. People stormed through them, each anxious to get a seat. Sister Geiser helped Helene to her feet, and slowly they followed behind the crowd. Peering into every car as they passed, they saw that the train was crammed. Finally they reached the last car.

"Will we be left behind?" Lotte asked.

"There. This one," Helene said. "There's a whole empty bench inside. Quickly, quickly." They loaded everyone on and gratefully sank onto the seats. The train pulled out of the station.

The top of the cars had carefully been draped with Red Cross flags to signal enemy pilots that this train was protected by international agreement and should not be attacked. But this was war, and treaties were broken on both sides of the conflict. Low-flying airplanes swooped down—some peppered the train with machine gun fire, while others threw hand grenades into the cars. Screaming women dragged their children under the wooden benches to protect them. People were wounded in every car—except the last one. There no bullet hit, no grenade exploded. Susi peacefully slept through the entire attack.

"God saved us a seat in this car," Helene said quietly.

Suddenly the planes turned and disappeared. Uninjured passengers bandaged and comforted the bleeding women and children while the train sat still for hours in the middle of nowhere. The journey began again at a snail's pace, and late at night the train rolled into the station closest to Eschenrod. It had taken all day to cover the 40-mile distance. A bus was waiting for them to take them on the last leg of the trip, and its engine roared to life as the families boarded.

In Eschenrod it was bitterly cold, and 18 inches of snow covered the ground. The commander of the transport, a high ranking League of Women officer, put the refugees in a schoolhouse several miles from the station, and from there assigned them to the different farmers. One of the women had seven children. They were quickly divided up between several homes.

"I do not wish to be separated from my children," Helene insisted. *If I am,* she thought to herself, *they'll have to eat pork, and they won't be able to keep the Sabbath.* She waited and waited in the schoolhouse, but no one was willing to take on a family of five. Finally all the placements had been made and only Helene, Sister Geiser, and the children remained.

In exasperation, the transport leader ordered the village innkeeper to provide a room for them over night till she was able to make more permanent arrangements the following day. Disgusted with the inconvenience, the landlady assigned them to a small upstairs room. It was bitterly cold. The water in the hand basin was frozen, and ice flowers bloomed on the windowpanes. The bedding was clammy, and when Helene tried to build a fire with the wet wood, it smoked and hissed but gave very little warmth. Susi, in her wet diapers, caught cold, and by morning was running a high fever and had difficulty breathing.

"Kurt," Helene said as she woke the weary boy the next morning, "they just told me that while the farmers are going to provide housing, we have to supply our own bedding and dishes. You'll have to go back to Frankfurt and get them."

Kurt set out right away, walking miles through the snow to the station. There he boarded the train for Frankfurt.

The train had no sooner pulled into the station when the air raid sirens went off, and bombs hailed out of the sky. The terrified boy sought shelter in the cellar of an already bombed out building. He huddled in a corner while the ground shook and fat rats scurried across the floor. When the attack stopped, he continued on the perilous journey to their home.

At the same time, back in Eschenrod, Helene heard an ominous droning in the sky. She stepped outside to see squadrons of enemy bombers flying in formation toward Frankfurt to drop their loads there.

"Lord," she prayed, interlinking her fingers and squeezing until her knuckles turned white, "will there never be an end to this horror? You have brought us safely so far. Will I now lose my boy in the inferno in Frankfurt and my baby to pneumonia? I have no more strength. Help us all."

CHAPTER 10

SAVED BY AN ANGEL

It was spring again, and another bitter winter was over.

Doing their best to gather their strength, the Wehrmacht penetrated further and further eastward into Russia. In their ruthless wake they left broken bodies and a broken country.

Ignoring Lieutenant Gutschalk's warnings, Franz tried to alleviate suffering wherever he could. Sometimes his own wounded or dying comrades needed assistance; at other times he aided Jews and Ukrainians. He did not distinguish between friend and foe, knowing that Jesus would have treated them the same also.

The Germans took hundreds of thousands of Russian soldiers prisoners-of-war. As Franz watched SS troops herd them to heavily guarded makeshift camps, his heart went out to these ragged, defeated men. They lived like cattle in the inadequate space, yet their misery had only begun. The Germans did not have enough food to feed their own men, much less the prisoners, and soon the camps became hellholes of starvation.

During a prolonged stay in one area, Franz learned that a prison camp was not far away. Though it was *streng verboten,* he visited the camp in the evening. On the way he thought, *So many things are strictly forbidden these days. I can't let that dictate my behavior.* When he arrived, it broke his heart to see the men beyond the barbed wire fence lift their skeletal hands to him in supplication.

He went to see his friend in the kitchen.

"Willi," he said urgently. "I have a special request. Would you let me have the leftover food after each meal?"

Willi stared long and hard at Franz. By this time he'd become used to his friend's unorthodox ways, so rolling his eyes he said, "OK, OK. Take anything you want. Just don't tell me what plot you are hatching now!"

Three times a day Franz covertly collected the scraps. In the evenings he made his way to the prison camp loaded with sacks of bread crusts and kettles of boiled potatoes and vegetables.

For several days he was unchallenged. Then the guard on duty spotted him, and approached him at a dead run.

"Stop!"

When he caught sight of Franz's rank insignia, he became more respectful. "What is your business here, Corporal?"

"I have left-over food that I am taking to the prisoners."

"I am sorry, Corporal, but this is strictly verboten."

"I know it is," Franz said earnestly. "But these men are humans like us. They are defenseless and at our mercy. What if you and I became prisoners-of-war to the Russians, and were hungry as wolves?"

The guard shuddered and crossed himself. "God forbid!"

"Wouldn't we be grateful if someone brought us food?"

The guard nodded. "You are right, of course. But I still can't allow it."

"Now listen," Franz said persuasively. "You are a guard. It is your duty to patrol. Just walk to the corner of the camp over there. While your back is turned, I'll toss the food over the fence, and by the time you come back, I'll be gone. You won't have seen me, and you won't be responsible."

Giving a quick "Heil Hitler" salute, the softhearted soldier turned without another word and resumed his patrol, knowing full well that he was risking his life by doing so.

Hastily, Franz threw the food over the fence. Falling on it like starved lions, the prisoners devoured what they could grasp. One man got hold of a boiled potato, and in his frenzy grabbed it so tight that the white mash squeezed through his fingers. Others seized his wrist and licked it off his hands. With pity Franz watched before stealing away. There was little hope for their survival. Of the 750,000 prisoners taken in Kiev alone, only 22,000 returned alive.

The war had gone on for four years. Franz missed his family and found it hard to live in a setting so foreign to his nature. His greatest satisfaction came when he had a chance to give Bible studies.

"Hasel," a curious soldier would ask, "how come you're so careful not to work on Saturday?"

"It's a long story. Come to my billet after supper, and I'll tell you."

Word spread to the other soldiers, and he had many opportunities to study the Bible truths and prophecies with the men. Eventually, there wasn't a soldier in the company who hadn't heard his witness. He found many of the men very open and interested, and he took them through an entire Bible study series.

At 8:00 one rainy Monday morning Sergeant Erich and other officers assembled in Franz's quarters to play skat, the men's favorite card game. Franz soon steered the conversation to Daniel's predictions about the Second Coming of Christ and the end of the world.

"Look at this," he said. He reached into his Bible pocket, produced a small postcard bearing a picture of the image in Daniel 2, and handed it around. Opening his Bible, he explained that these were the last days of earth's history.

"Hitler will never be able to unite the world under German rule," he said confidently, "because that is not in harmony with Bible prophecy. The next event will be the rock that will smash the statue, and that will mark the end of our world. Then God will set up His own kingdom."

Fascinated, the men listened, asking many questions. Franz always seemed to find the right response.

Finally someone glanced at the clock.

"It's noon! We've been sitting here talking for four hours. We're going to have to rush if we want to get anything to eat!"

In the officer's mess, the men enthusiastically shared with others what they had just heard. It didn't take long for word to reach Hauptmann Miekus, who had replaced Brandt two years earlier. He didn't waste any time summoning Franz to his quarters at 1:00 p.m.

"Hasel." There was an unfamiliar growl in his voice. Though normally well disposed toward Franz, he was clearly indignant this time. "Is it true that you talked to my officers for four hours about the end of the world?"

"Yes, sir, I did."

"How dare you say such things?"

"Sir?"

"You know perfectly well that Hitler is establishing the Third Reich. That Reich will last 1,000 years!"

Franz stood looking at him, not quite sure what to say.

"There is not going to be an end to the world, Hasel!" Hauptmann Miekus stood to his feet, and pointed his finger firmly at Franz. "I barely managed to defend you to my officers this time. But I absolutely forbid you to talk about it again. Do you understand?"

"Yes, sir." Franz said, with a deferential hand-to-cap salute.

"I just hope," said Miekus, half to himself, as Franz turned away, "that you haven't shared this nonsense with the troops yet."

If only you knew, thought Franz. He left the room, leaving the Hauptmann shaking his head. For two years now all German military personnel had been ordered to salute only with a stiffly outstretched arm and a crisp *"Heil Hitler!"* Somehow the incorrigible Corporal Hasel always ignored this.

In his worship that night, Franz again turned to Amos 5:13: "Therefore the prudent man keeps quiet in such times, for the times are evil" (NIV). He heeded this advice and determined to become much more cautious when talking to the soldiers. But still he never missed an appropriate opportunity to tell about Christ, His Second Coming, and accountability to God.

During the past years he had earned the respect of most of the men. Only a few of them—mostly the newcomers—ridiculed him. Leo, who had recently joined the Pioneers, was the worst. He fancied himself a comedian, and used Franz as the butt of his jokes.

"Hey, Franz," he would shout. "You're turning yellow from eating all those carrots!"

Another time, he would hoot with laughter. "Reading the Bible again, Hasel? We'll have to put you in a zoo with our ancestors, the apes!"

Finally, Franz's patience snapped.

"Leo," he said in what he hoped was a deadly voice. "I warn you. If you make fun of me one more time, I'll beat you up!"

Everyone within hearing immediately turned to watch.

Leo measured Franz with his eyes. *Hasel's tall,* he seemed to be thinking, *but he works in the office all day, while I'm out building bridges. I can take him, easy.*

"Come on then, Hasel," he sneered, "I'm not scared of a cabbage-eater's punch."

With one mighty swing of his fist, Franz knocked Leo unconscious, landing him four feet away in the mud. Franz brushed his hands together in a gesture that said louder than words, "There, I showed you!"

His comrades whistled and cheered. The luckless Leo, still out like a light, had no way of knowing what they knew: though nearly twice the age of most of the younger men, Franz regularly won the weight lifting competitions.

But as Leo began coming to his senses, Franz was coming to his. He knew what he had to do. First he went into his office and knelt by his desk.

"Lord," he prayed, "I have sinned against Leo and against You. I trusted in my own strength rather than listening to Your guidance. What a hypocrite I am, talking to the men about a Christlike life while acting like a common street brawler. I don't want to be this kind of person. Please forgive me."

Then Franz went outside and apologized to Leo, who by now was sitting up trying to clear his head. While this incident gained Franz the admiration of many of the soldiers, he was ashamed of his behavior. He did not want respect that was based on violence.

Meanwhile, the German infantry captured a village containing a railroad junction deep in the heart of the Ukraine not far from where the Pioneers were stationed. Franz and five other soldiers were sent ahead to this town with orders to prepare living quarters for the rest of the unit, who would join them in a few days. Since no danger was expected, Franz was also asked to take along the company documents, all the money, and the goods from the store. They took a jeep and a truck with a trailer, loaded them high with supplies, and set out.

When they arrived at the junction, they found men from other battalions already stationed there. Just opposite the train station, Franz discovered a building, which the locals considered to be a hotel. Its rooms had dirt floors, and were stripped of all furniture. Outside were an outhouse and a water well. Deciding to stay in one of the unoccupied rooms, he threw his straw tick on the floor and piled the document files into a corner. The others found a barn where they made their beds on hay.

Since this was an important junction, everyone had to be watchful. Twice a day Franz climbed the wooden observation tower attached to the train station and scanned the horizon. At night the soldiers slept fully clothed except for their boots. Things were quiet, however, and it was easy to let vigilance slip.

On Friday, when done with his bookkeeping, Franz polished his boots and brushed his uniform, as was his custom on the preparation day. By sundown he was ready to celebrate the Sabbath. He decided to spend the next day in the woods not far away. Here he would be undisturbed in his Bible study and meditation. Every day he'd been conscientiously reading his Bible and praying, but he'd known for quite awhile that he needed some quiet time alone with the Lord. Ever since the incident with Leo, God seemed somehow far away.

Sabbath morning at breakfast he took extra slices of bread and left, carrying his Bible in one pocket and the bread and a canister of water in the other.

I wonder if it's worth the risk, he asked himself. *When I'm separated from the unit, I'm more vulnerable. A sniper could pick me off, and no one would find me. I could step on a land mine and be blown to bits. Should I stay in my billet?*

No, he finally decided. *I have to go. I need to regain my closeness to God.*

In the woods, he found a broken log to sit on and opened his Bible. Almost immediately he was distracted by a squirrel scolding in the branches above him. He brought his eyes back to the page.

"In the world ye shall have tribulation . . ."

A crow cawed loudly. He followed it with his eyes, then jerked his attention back to Scripture. Maybe he needed to read a different passage.

"He that dwelleth in the secret place of the Most High shall abide under the shadow of the Almighty . . ."

He couldn't keep his thoughts on what he was reading. Strange that he should feel so empty. Was the war getting to him? He was worried— no, worse than that. He was afraid. Not of snipers or landmines or Hitler. He was afraid because even though he had disciplined himself to read the Bible daily, he no longer heard God speaking to him. He had lost the sense of God's presence.

Now, sitting there alone in the forest, more than 1,000-plus miles away from his family, he felt a deep depression settle on him. As the day wore on, he became more and more discouraged. He felt as far from God as he ever had.

Finally, before going back to camp, he prayed, "Lord, You see the state of mind I'm in. If You are still with me, then give me a sign."

On the way back to camp Franz sang the words of the ancient hymn: "And though this world, with devils filled, should threaten to undo us, we will not fear, for God hath willed His truth to triumph through us. . . ."

Two weeks went by, during which the Soviets steadily stepped up their offensive. Daily Russian tanks advanced toward the village, and just as often were driven back by German Stukas bombarding them from the air. Each side hurled grenades, fired shells, and blasted each other with artillery. The shooting was incessant. When their unit did not join them, the six Pioneers felt more and more uneasy.

Another Sabbath passed. Now, of course, there was no chance of a quiet day in the woods, so Franz remained by himself in his bare dirt-floor room. As he paged through his Bible his eyes fell on familiar words from Psalm 91: "He will command his angels concerning you to guard you in all your ways; they will lift you up in their hands, so that you will not strike your foot against a stone." He'd read them often, but in his mood of spiritual emptiness they seemed distant and impersonal. Finally, as evening came, he fell into a heavy sleep.

Early the next morning he awoke with a start. Something was not right. He lay still for a moment. Then he heard it: a low, rumbling drone, very far away.

Thunder? He wondered drowsily. *No, it can't be thunder. It sounds too steady, too—human.*

Human?

He leaped out of bed, jumped into his boots, and dashed out of the room and across the dirt road to the observation tower. Scrambling up the stairs two at a time, he eventually reached the top. The ominous rumbling was louder up here, and as he peered out into the early dawn he could just make out the shadowy bulks of Russian tanks converging on the village from all directions. Other, closer vehicles scurried away—the German infantry was fleeing posthaste.

They've got us, Franz thought. *This is it. This is the end. Dear God, help us. Are we lost?*

He glanced around. *No! One road is open yet! That's our only hope.*

Franz clattered down the stairs and bolted across the village square to the barn.

"Up, up!" he shouted to the other Pioneers. "The Russians are coming! Leave everything and get out now! Take the road to the south. It's our only chance."

The others poured out of the building. They cranked up the jeep and truck, while Franz rushed to his quarters. There in his room was the soldiers' pay, to be given to the men on Wednesday. In those document files were top-secret bulletins about future moves of the German army. His standing orders were to burn everything rather than let it fall into enemy hands. But there was no time.

What am I going to do? Franz wondered desperately. Options and objections tumbled through his mind. *This door doesn't even have a lock. If I stay behind, I'm sure to be killed or taken prisoner. In my holster I have nothing but a boot-polish-blackened piece of wood. And even if I did have a real weapon, what could one lone soldier do to defend these documents? Yet I'm ultimately responsible for them, and if the Russians find our plans and use them, I'll be court-martialed as a traitor and executed.*

He grabbed a piece of chalk and left the room, banging the door after him. Outside, he drew a skull and crossbones on the door. Underneath, he wrote in huge letters,

DANGER!
MINES—DO NOT ENTER!

Then he dashed away to where the huge diesel truck, pulling its trailer, was driving off. The little jeep scuttled on ahead. In the commotion his comrades hadn't noticed that he was left behind. With a running leap, Franz landed on the connecting tow bar and clung to the coupling, trying desperately to keep his balance while the truck bounced over potholes, scattering mud and gravel.

"We are going to make it," he prayed aloud. "Thank you, Lord."

But from where he was riding Franz couldn't see an approaching curve. The driver made a sharp right turn, and the truck bed angled toward

Franz and toppled him from his perch. He landed on the road, his head two feet from the front wheel of the trailer.

In that flash of time he knew that the wheel was going to crush his head. His entire life passed before his eyes like a movie, beginning with that moment and going all the way back to the time when, as a 2-year-old, he had fallen down the cellar stairs on his grandparents' farm.

So this, not battle, is the end. Save me, Lord! Forgive my sins! Watch over my family.

The wheel touched his skull. Franz closed his eyes waiting for the final crushing impact.

Just then, someone grabbed him by the collar of his uniform, wrenched him away from the wheel, and with one gigantic lifting movement, deposited him on the very top of the trailer. For a moment he sprawled there, dazed and shaking. Then he lifted his head and looked around to find his rescuer and thank him.

There was no one there.

Trembling, almost sobbing, with relief, Franz thanked God for giving him the sign he had prayed for. Awed, he remembered the words that had seemed so impersonal to him on Sabbath: "He will command his angels concerning you to guard you in all your ways; they will lift you up in their hands" (Ps. 91:11, 12, NIV).

Soon the vehicles reached a wooded area where they hid for the day. In the distance they heard the crackling of rifle fire, and every once in a while they felt the earth tremble from the force of tremendous explosions.

"Wait a minute," one of the men said. "What's happening? You saw our side retreating, didn't you, Hasel?"

"Exactly," Franz replied in a puzzled voice. "There are no Germans left to fight the Russians, yet it sounds like some sort of battle going on over there."

By late afternoon the entire countryside had become eerily silent, and they ventured back. Low-crawling to a safe vantage point, they peered down on a road clogged with a whole line of Russian tanks. There was no sign of life.

"Watch out," whispered one of Franz's companions. "It could be a trap."

"Right," said another. "It's happened before. Whole units have been lured into ambushes just like this."

Suddenly they saw a movement.

"It's all right," someone shouted. "I'm German. Don't shoot."

A lone soldier appeared and walked toward them.

"Who are you?" they shouted suspiciously.

He grinned weakly, and they could see his face was pale. "My name is Hans Kessler."

"Where's your unit?"

"Gone."

"You were left behind?"

"That's right. I belong to a Panzerabwehrbattalion. When the Russians attacked, my unit took off before I knew they were going. I grabbed my little anti-tank gun and ran along the road trying to catch up, but I realized right away that I'd never reach them. So I decided to hide behind a thick hedge beside the road.

"From where I was hiding, I saw the Russians enter the town and ransack all the buildings. When they found no soldiers, they got back in their tanks again and started heading down this road in my direction, because that's the direction the Germans had gone.

"They couldn't see me behind the hedge. And I was ready for them. In my training I'd learned that Russian tanks are heavily armored in the front and on the sides but pretty much unprotected in the rear. So I just waited for each tank to pass by me, and then I fired a round at its ammunition chamber located in the back—and of course it went up with a roar.

"Well, this must have driven the Russians stark crazy. All they could see was tank after tank bursting into a ball of flames. They couldn't tell where on earth the attack was coming from, so I guess they just panicked. They brought the whole line of tanks to a halt, and they just abandoned them and ran helter-skelter across the fields."

For single-handedly driving the Russians back, Hans Kessler later received the Iron Cross 1st and 2nd class. And a promotion.

"Well," said Franz after hearing the astonishing story, "I guess there's nothing to keep us from going back to the town."

When they arrived back at their quarters, they found all their belongings destroyed or stolen. What the Russians were not able to take, they had torn up, then bayoneted and trampled. Nothing could be salvaged.

Jaws clenched with apprehension, Franz jogged over to the room where he'd left the money and documents. He paused outside the door for a second or two, dreading to enter.

But when he finally opened the door, he found the room undisturbed. The records and secret orders were all in place. The soldiers' pay was where he had left it. God had sent His angels here too.

CHAPTER 11

IN ESCHENROD

While Kurt was struggling to get to their apartment in Frankfurt, the inn's landlady curtly said to Helene, "I just can't keep you in my house with your four children. Follow me, and I will show you a place where you can live."

She led her across the street through deep snow to an old washhouse. Once a week, the peasant women used to light fires here under the huge caldrons to boil their laundry. Now the building had fallen into disrepair and was no longer used. It consisted of an empty room with a cement floor. The damp walls were covered with ice, and icicles hung from the ceiling. There was one small broken window; the door was missing. An open latrine sat in one corner giving off an overpowering stench.

Seeing Helene's horrified expression the woman said, "What's the matter? Don't you like it? Just be grateful I am giving you this much! I have nothing else for you!"

Through the open door the landlady yelled, "Jacques, Jacques, haul some straw in here. Get a move on, you dirty, lazy pig!"

A young man, captured in France and transported to Germany to do slave labor, appeared on the porch of the inn followed by the landlord, who kicked him down the steps with a curse, then hit him with a whip across his back as he landed in the street. Helene ran to the youth and helped him up, brushing the snow off him. Then she went back to her icy room.

For the first time in all the years of the war, she gave in to despair. In the bone-chilling cold she sat on the bed and cried as if her heart would break. Seeing their strong, courageous mother in tears terrified Lotte and Gerd. Silently they stood by her side, not knowing how to comfort her.

There came a soft knock. Jacques stood in the door with a steaming pot of Ersatzkaffee, a coffee substitute made from roasted grain.

"You are good woman," he said in broken German. "Landlady nicht good. I help you."

Gratefully, Helene and the children drank, feeling warmed not only by the hot liquid but also the young man's kindness.

Later Sister Geiser arrived. She had been assigned to another family, and had come by to see how her friends were faring. Helene's account infuriated her.

"Pull yourself together," she ordered. "We are going to pay a visit to the Nazi leader in the village."

They burst in on Herr Schaefer just as he sat down to have breakfast with the League of Women officer in charge of the evacuation transport. His table was laden with sausage, ham, butter, bread, cake, coffee, and milk till it could hold no more. There were always plenty of provisions for Party leaders.

"What do you want?" he asked rather ungraciously.

The evacuation officer was even more belligerent. "How dare you barge in here like this?" she bellowed. "Get out, get out right now!"

Tiny Sister Geiser stood her ground, her feet firmly planted apart, her fists on her hips.

"Now you listen to me," she said in a voice of deadly calm. "If you think that that wash house is a fit accommodation for a family, you can go live there yourself. I wouldn't put an animal in a place like that!" She gestured toward Helene. "This woman here has four children, and her youngest is just a nursing infant. They have had no food for two days while you sit here gorging yourself.

"Tell me something," she said, glowering at the evacuation officer. "Do you have a husband?"

Dumbfounded by this display of audacity, the female officer sputtered, "Yes I do. What is that to you?"

"Is he at home?"

"Yes. But this conversation is over," the officer said quickly. "I order you to leave immediately!"

"Oh, no, you don't," Sister Geiser continued fearlessly, never budging. "What we need to do is to send your husband to the front and bring the father of these four children home so he can take care of his family. That would be justice!" She stood as tall as she possibly could, and rapped out her final words with all the authority of a storm trooper. "If you don't resolve this situation in short order, I will report you to the authorities—if I have to go all the way to Adolf Hitler himself. As you know, he promotes big families, and supports women with children."

Behind the officer's back, the party leader frantically gestured to Sister Geiser to leave. He indicated that he would follow soon. Majestically, Sister Geiser took Helene's arm and led her from the room.

Two hours later, Herr Schaefer did indeed arrive in Helene's freezing quarters. He shook her hand and apologized for the hardships she had gone through. Helene sensed right away that he had a kind heart.

"Frau Hasel," he said, "I have personally visited all the farmers in the village. "No one wants to take you with four children. But the peasant women all tell me that you are doing right not to be separated from them. They would do the same. Children belong with their mother."

Helene nodded. Yet her heart sank at these discouraging words.

"But," he said, "I have found a possible home for you. It is an old couple, the Josts, who are in their seventies. Because of their age they are not actually required to take any evacuees. But they feel sorry for you, and would like to meet you before they make a decision."

Together Herr Schaefer and Helene went to the Josts' house. Old Herr Jost was seated on a bench by their tiled stove, and his wife sat at their table. Frau Jost's face was as wrinkled as a prune. She had her gray hair done up in a topknot, and in her mouth there was only one tooth.

With their gentle expressions they looked like the ideal grandparents. As they silently looked each other over, Helene took an immediate liking to them. *Thanks be to God,* she thought. *Here's where I want to stay. Please, dear Lord, let it be.*

Frau Jost spoke first. "Frau Hasel, no one wants to take you with your children. That is hard. I'll keep you. The other families should be ashamed of themselves."

She smiled tentatively. "I just hope we get along," she said. "We have never had children of our own, and now we are old, and we like a quiet life. I suppose there will be a lot of noise?"

"No, no," Helene assured her. "I'll make sure the children won't disturb you. If they want to make noise, they can go outside. I am so glad you are giving us shelter."

"Well then," Frau Jost said kindly, "you are welcome here."

Herr Jost got up from his bench. "Move in right away," he said heartily. "Consider this your home. Bring the children. I like children." With moist eyes he shook Helene's hand.

Helene bundled up the children, and Jacques helped carry their baggage as they moved in. Frau Jost had already built a fire in the wood stove in their room. so that by the time they arrived, the room was nice and warm.

"Come in, come in," she said. "I have a pan of chamomile tea boiling on the stove. Maybe it will put some moisture in the air to help the baby breathe easier." Sure enough, over the next few days Susi completely recovered.

Late in the evening Kurt arrived safely with their bedding and dishes, and they felt even more at home.

It was indeed the beginning of better times. Daily Frau Jost provided butter, eggs, bread, and cream. When she baked a cake, she gave them some—in fact there was nothing this dear couple had that they did not share with their lodgers.

Helene showed her gratitude by vigorously cleaning the house from top to bottom till it shone, and even swept the street outside while the children herded the cattle and helped on the farm. It seemed that no job was too hard for them to accomplish. Frau Jost often said to Helene, "Frau Hasel, God sent you to me!"

It wasn't long before the neighbors began to notice this flurry of activity. Their own evacuees didn't stir a finger to help them, and one by one they began to sidle up to Helene in the street.

"Frau Hasel, how are you?"

"Fine, thank you," Helene said as she plied her broom.

"I want you to know that I would be happy to have you and your family in my home. I have space available now. You would have a much bigger room than the Josts can provide."

Politely, Helene declined. "The Josts took us when nobody else wanted us," she said. "They understood our needs, and they treated us with kindness. We are very happy there, and we are going to stay."

The Josts were devout Lutherans, and on Sundays they went to the only church in the village. When Frau Jost donned her regional costume— a white blouse with big puffed sleeves, a black velvet skirt, a rustling taffeta apron, a colorful silk shawl, and little black velvet slippers—she looked like a picture right out of a travel book.

Since there were no Adventists to worship with, Helene accompanied them regularly. The pastor had been drafted, but had appointed a simple peasant to lead the church in his absence. Though this man had little education, Helene was often deeply moved by the powerful sermons he preached.

Once a week a group of women gathered at the Jost house for Bible studies. The pastor's wife took a great liking to Helene.

"Come live with me, Frau Hasel."

Helene laughed. "Have you done your addition? Between you and me we would have nine children in the house. We wouldn't survive it!" Chuckling, they discarded that idea.

One day Helene heard that a truck would be going to Frankfurt to pick

In 1917 Franz Hasel (far left, middle row) served in World War I with the Pioneer Unit, the same outfit into which he was drafted in 1939.

The Hasel family, shown here in Vienna, Austria, in 1936, couldn't know that in three years Papa Franz would be drafted, and that all would suffer for their faith. From left: Lotte, Helene, Kurt, Franz, and Gerhard (nicknamed Gerd).

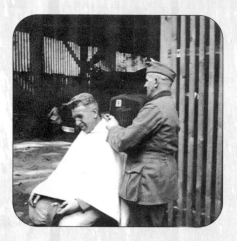

Forty-year-old Franz was one of the first draftees into Hitler's Wehrmacht. Here he good-naturely submits to a "shearing" by a military barber.

During basic training Franz discovered, to his horror, that he was an excellent sharpshooter. This led him to take dramatic steps to make sure he would never kill a human being.

Because of typing and accounting skills he had honed as an Adventist publishing director, Franz was promoted to corporal and became first company clerk. Here, standing behind the cash box, he pays wages to the soldiers of Pioneer Park Company 699.

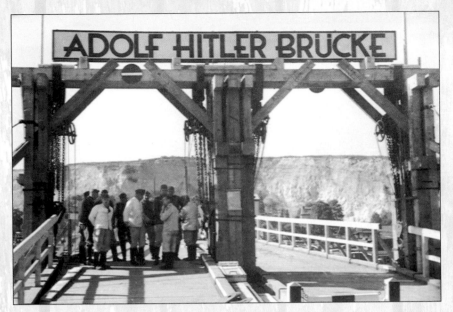

A few months after the war began Pioneer Park Company 699 built this sturdy Brücke (bridge) across the Rhine and dedicated it to the Führer.

As the German Army swept through France, Poland, and Russia, Franz often entered hastily abandoned dwellings like this one. It was in just such a house that he "looted"—and later remorsefully returned—a small spool of sewing machine thread.

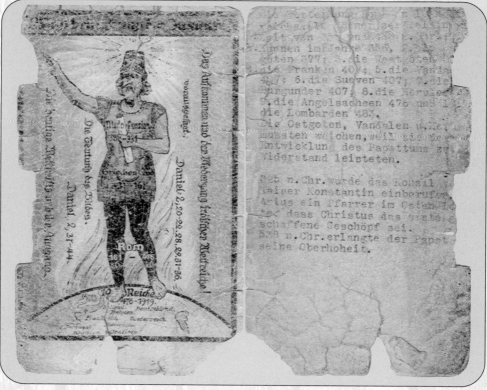

When Franz was baptized in 1921, he was given this postcard picture of the image of Daniel 2, on the back of which he typed explanatory notes. He carried this card throughout the war, and used it to explain to other soldiers—including on one occasion his commanding officer—why Hitler couldn't possibly win!

The faces of peace and war: on the left is the smiling Franz Hasel, conference publishing director in 1936. Six years later it's 1942, and Corporal Hasel is in the Ukraine. His tense, watchful gaze betrays the pressures faced by a frontline soldier.

Tante Fischer in 1964.

As the war continued, Frankfurt became too dangerous for Helene and the children. An Adventist woman they affectionately called Tante (Aunt) Fischer gave them refuge in her Black Forest home.

Papa Franz's furloughs were few and brief, and the family made the most of them. Here, in 1940, they take a walk to the "Bird Paradise," their favorite Sabbath afternoon destination, which they'd visited on the very day Franz received his draft notice.

At first being Black Forest war refugees was something of an adventure for the Hasel children, especially when it involved surprises like the feisty little black kitten Peter, held here by Kurt.

Kurt (top), Lotte (middle), and Gerhard (bottom), attended Frankfurt's Ludwig Richter School, where Anne and Margot Frank had been students a few years earlier. Kurt and Gerd are holding chalk pencils and writing on slates to conserve paper.

Helene and the children in front of the Frankfurt apartment building where they lived. The year is 1943. Miraculously, this building and five others in the same block survived the intense bombing that leveled 80 percent of the city.

In 1944, 14-year-old Kurt began to feel the pressure to join the Hitler Youth. At that time the Youth were involved in community service and bombing cleanup work, so Helene allowed Kurt to enlist, thinking that this might be a legitimate way to cooperate with the government. Almost as soon as Kurt got used to his new uniform, however, Sabbath work became a problem, and he was forced to flee to the country.

Shown here in 1936, a radiant Kurt plays with one of his favorite toys—a castle and some soldiers. When he and his family evacuated to the country during the bombing, they had to leave everything behind. When they returned, the windows of their ground-floor apartment had been blown out by bomb blasts, and the whole neighborhood had been pillaged by looters. Yet all the family's belongings, including the soldiers and castle, were still there.

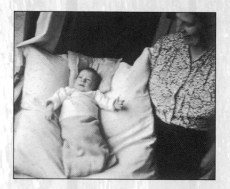

Truly a war baby, Susi was born late one night in 1943. Three hours later as air-raid sirens sounded, a weak and exhausted Helene had to hurry through the darkness with her newborn and the rest of the children to a tightly crowded bomb shelter.

One of the postwar "miracle boxes" from America contained this beautiful dress and red sweater for Susi, who was just starting school.

The surprise gift for Susi after her worn-out red sweater had mysteriously disappeared.

up some furniture for the evacuees. Helene got permission from Party leader Herr Schaefer to go in with the driver and bring some of her things back.

"You're going to Frankfurt, Frau Hasel?" asked Frau Jost. "Would you be willing to do me a favor? If I packed a basket with farm produce, would you take it there and trade it for some cotton fabric and maybe some other things I can't get in the village?"

"Certainly," Helene replied.

Soon the older woman had her basket ready. On top she spread a thick layer of moss into which she carefully bedded 50 fresh eggs. Then she covered everything with hay and securely fastened burlap over the top.

Helene and Kurt climbed into the back of the truck and settled on some sacks of flour. At a sharp curve in the road, Kurt lost his balance and landed full force on the basket. Hearing the crack, Helene knew the eggs were crushed. She was afraid to look. *Dear Lord,* she prayed, *what is Frau Jost going to say? Would it be asking too much of You to please make these eggs whole again?*

When they got to Frankfurt, it turned out that there was no room for their furniture after all, and no time to do any trading. When they returned late at night, the truck stopped at the neighboring village where some other people's furniture was unloaded. Then the driver took Helene and Kurt to Eschenrod.

"Where is our basket?" she asked the driver.

He rolled his eyes. "Sorry," he said. "I must have unloaded it along with the furniture. Don't worry. Tomorrow I'll go back there and get it, and I'll drop if off by your back door."

The next day Helene checked the back door periodically, but there was no basket. She explained to Frau Jost what had happened as best she could, but she could see that the woman did not believe her.

Every morning when she heard the delivery truck, Helene sneaked out the back door hoping to see the basket. Each time she ran into Frau Jost in her nightgown doing the same thing! Helene would chuckle, but Frau Jost didn't see the humorous side of it.

"What is going on with my basket?" she asked rather snippily. "I am beginning to think that you are telling me a big story. Did you sell the food in Frankfurt and make a lot of money?"

Helene's conscience was clear, but she wondered what Frau Jost would say when she finally got her basket back and discovered the eggs were crushed. She stopped checking the door.

After a week, Frau Jost knocked softly on Helene's door calling, "Frau Hasel, the basket is here. Come and help me unpack it."

With dread in her heart Helene hastily dressed and went to the parlor. On the way she prayed again, *Lord, please make those eggs whole again.*

Frau Jost had already taken off the sacking that covered the basket. Now she carefully removed the hay and moss she had used for packing. One by one, she took out the eggs.

Not one was broken.

"Frau Hasel," said the older woman, "I am sorry that I doubted you. I will not distrust you again."

One day soon afterward, a band of Polish prisoners-of-war was marched into the village. A dirty, ragged little boy limped along beside them. The mayor assigned the crippled child to live with the Josts and help them on the farm.

Frau Jost immediately enlisted Helene's help. "I would like to take Adam to church with us on Sunday," she said. "But he needs to be cleaned up first. I have no experience with such things. Could you help me?"

Helene got warm water and a big bowl. First, she vigorously shampooed his hair, then set him in the sunshine to let it dry while she barbered it. Meanwhile, under Helene's direction, Frau Jost had set up the zinc bathtub, filled it with hot water, and added soda to it.

"This boy," Frau Jost muttered darkly, "has not had a bath in months. Once he'd removed his soiled clothes, she gingerly picked them up, took them outside, and burned them. His skin was so caked with filth that he had to soak in the hot water awhile before they could scrub it off.

Adam's fingernails were long and shiny, and curved out beyond the ends of his fingertips like claws. He patiently endured the shampooing and soaking and scraping. He protested only once—when they wanted to cut away an old string he wore around his neck. He refused to let them even touch it.

"Frau Jost, look at his feet," Helene said. "Do you have scissors?"

Adam's toenails had grown like talons, completely curling around the tip of his toes and under again. The scissors were not strong enough to cut them.

"I have some garden shears," she said doubtfully.

"That might do it."

Sure enough, the shears did the trick—and worked a small miracle. Because when Adam emerged from the tub clean and shiny, and stepped onto the floor, he wasn't crippled at all! It was the long toenails that had made walking almost impossible for him.

Helene brought out some baby lotion and gently smoothed it over his chapped skin. Then she brought him some of Kurt's clothing—underwear, a shirt, a pair of pants, shoes, and socks. Frau Jost found a small wool vest that fit him. Every Sunday thereafter, Adam accompanied them to church, and so great was the transformation that the other Poles did not even recognize him until Adam waved and called to them.

At 12, Adam was small and emaciated for his age. He worked very hard, however, and soon picked up fragments of German so he could communicate with them. He was far from lazy, but often he came down late for breakfast.

"I wonder what's keeping him," Frau Jost said to Helene one morning. "I'm going upstairs to peek through the keyhole." She returned a few minutes later. "What do you know? Adam is kneeling by his bed, praying the rosary."

He seemed to yearn for other things from his young past, because at sunset he stood by the garden gate and gazed into the distance. "Adam home, Adam home there," he said, sadly pointing east.

Frau Jost accepted another Polish refugee into her home, a young man named Josef. She'd given him a niche in the wall across from Helene's room where he could sleep. While other German peasants treated Poles like animals, and half-starved them, Josef ate with Frau Jost and Helene's family at the table.

Since Helene had no closet space, she pounded a nail in the wall of the hallway and hung one of Papa's good woolen suits there. She often stored leftover food on top of an old ornate chest in the corridor. Josef never touched anything.

"Josef," she offered, "if you would ever like to go to church or to a dance, you are welcome to wear the suit that's hanging here."

Though dressed in rags and very poor, Josef shook his head. "The suit belongs to your husband. I not wear it. Thank you, thank you."

Josef told them a little about Adam's background. His father and older brother had fallen at the front. Only his mother and 2-year-old sister were left. Then his mother contracted tuberculosis. Before she died, she tied a little medallion with a picture of Mary and Jesus around his neck. It was Adam's only keepsake of his mother. After her death, someone took the little girl, but Adam was left to wander the streets. That's where the soldiers found him and took him along to Germany. Frau Jost's tender heart was touched. Quietly she made plans for Adam's future.

One morning Helene looked out the window and saw Adam already busy in the garden. But he was behaving strangely.

"What's he doing out there?" she asked Frau Jost.

The other woman came and looked out the window. "He looks doubled over," she said. "He's just wandering down the vegetable rows looking under every leaf."

After Adam had gone through the garden, he went into the yard and carefully inspected the ground.

"Oh, no," said Helene. "Remember that medallion around his neck? That old string must have broken, and he's lost his only treasure. Lotte! Kurt! Gerd! Come here!"

Soon the whole family, Herr and Frau Jost included, turned the house and yard and barn upside down. They even examined the outhouse. But to no avail. The medallion was lost, and Adam was inconsolable. Late at night, they heard him sobbing into his pillow.

A few days later Frau Jost decided to replace the straw in Adam's mattress. When she shook out the tick, she heard something clink. Sure enough, it was the precious medallion. It must have come off in the night and fallen into the straw. Excitedly, she called for Adam, and when he saw the shiny object in her hand, he burst into tears and kissed it fervently. Hanging it from a sturdy new string, he soon carried it around his neck again.

Since the Josts had no heirs, they decided to adopt Adam and leave the farm to him. But when Josef explained his good fortune to the boy, he shook his head sadly and said he could not accept it, because after the war he must go back home and find his little sister. The Josts understood, and loved him even more for his devotion to his family.

Yet not far from these gentle family scenes, Nazi ugliness raised its head. About 12 miles from Eschenrod was a camp of the SS, Hitler's elite forces. Fifty German girls worked there as secretaries. All were blond, blue-eyed, and beautiful. It was rumored that the Nazis were getting them pregnant as part of the effort to create an Aryan super race.

When it became obvious that the war would be lost, the SS shot the girls to keep them from revealing their secrets and tossed them into a hastily dug mass grave. The Americans discovered this and ordered the Germans to dig them up and bury them properly. In turn, the Germans ordered the Poles to do this unpleasant task.

When the Americans arrived and liberated the Poles, the latter saw their chance to revenge themselves for the degradation and inhumane treatment they had suffered at the hands of the Germans. One day they engaged in a spree of looting and destruction that left little behind. They herded off pigs, chickens, rabbits. They tore vegetables out of the gardens and trampled them, slashed clothes hanging on the line to dry, and ripped haystacks apart and scattered the hay.

The next morning, Frau Jost noticed with wonder that none of her things had been touched. And Helene's clothes were still fluttering in the wind.

CHAPTER 12

IN THE CAUCASUS

Meanwhile the fighting on the Eastern front accelerated. The Wehrmacht had sent replacements for fallen soldiers, and the army launched an offensive that was a huge success: the Russians were pushed back. In the south the Germans crossed the Volga, and this freed the Pioneers to finally leave the Donetz basin where they had been for several months. The orders were to keep moving east.

One afternoon while Franz was busy reconciling accounts, the mail brought orders for the Pioneers to turn quickly toward Stalingrad. Hitler was sending his 6th Army there to conquer and watch this important city, and Pioneers would help by building bridges and smoothing out rough dirt roads.

Franz ran to the Hauptmann carrying the orders.

"Stalingrad!" the Hauptmann said after studying them. "I don't have a good feeling about this. I hear that the city is a stronghold of the Soviet army. I'm afraid we're going to lose many men there." He sighed and handed Franz the orders to file. "But I guess there's nothing to be done. Orders are orders."

The Pioneers started moving and soon crossed the eastern border of the Ukraine into Russia itself. They reached the city of Rostov, when suddenly the orders changed.

"Erich, look at this," Franz called excitedly across the room to the sergeant, who had just entered. "We are no longer going to Stalingrad but to the Caucasus!"

Erich glanced at the document, "Man, this is good news. Stalingrad is a hell!" He looked speculatively at Franz, "I don't suppose this has anything to do with your God. Is He looking out for you again?"

The Pioneers changed their course, crossed the river Don, and headed southeast to the Caucasus Mountains. Much later they learned that the 6th army in Stalingrad had been almost completely destroyed in the worst battle of World War II.

Soon the Pioneers reached the vast Kalmykia steppe, a semi-arid grass-covered plain reaching all the way to the Caspian Sea. As they cautiously began their march across, they came upon small settlements where the people seemed centuries behind modern civilization. They still lit fires by striking two flints together until a spark set some dry shreds of moss to smoldering. When the soldiers pulled out their cigarette lighters, pushed a button, and produced instant flames, the people stared in disbelief.

For several days the German soldiers found so little water that the precious supply had to be rationed. In the morning each man received one tin cup full of slightly brackish water, which was all he had to wash, shave, and brush his teeth with. Franz developed a system that worked quite efficiently. He dipped his toothbrush into the water, brushed his teeth and rinsed them with a large mouthful of water. This he spit back into the cup. Then he wet his shaving brush, lathered his face, and shaved. Finally, he wet his hands with the now soapy water and wiped them over his face and neck. By then not a drop was left.

Halfway across the Kalmykia steppe, the Pioneers came to a halt near a large wooden marker that proclaimed in several languages: "You are standing on the border between Europe and Asia." They decided to camp there for the night. Somehow being in the shadow of that sign made them realize how very far away from home they were.

Late that night Franz stepped out of his tent. There was no moon—only the stars sparkled brightly in the velvet sky. They seemed close enough to touch.

Looking up at them, he wondered where his loved ones were. Were they still alive? Maybe at that moment they also were looking up at the sky and thinking about him. And he knew that the same God who watched over the stars in their course was also watching over him and his family. Reassured, he returned to his tent.

Finally the company reached the Caucasus. Having come from the desert-like steppe, they felt like they had arrived in Eden. Far below the icy summits of its mountain range, grapevines and pomegranates hung heavy with fruit. The water was fresh and sweet. Mountain meadows bloomed with wild flowers.

Best of all, the people were friendly, welcoming the Germans as liberators from Communist rule. They gladly gave the soldiers the best quarters, and willingly bartered goods with the men. For the time being the Pioneers were stationed in the shadow of Mount Elbrus, at 18,510 feet the highest mountain in Europe.

During this quiet interlude Franz received an official-looking letter from the government of the state of Bavaria. He could not imagine what it was about.

Glancing at the postmark, he saw that the letter had been in transit for more than four months before reaching him. As he slit the envelope open and started reading, he suddenly remembered.

More than eight years earlier, he'd spent some time in the Catholic city of Passau, in Bavaria, selling the book *The Desire of Ages* from door to door. A priest had falsely accused him of misrepresenting the contents of the book and misleading the Catholic people, and the authorities had imprisoned him. When his case went to court, he was found innocent of the charges, but in spite of the verdict, the judge still sentenced him to eight years probation.

And now, finally, he held in his hands the letter from the Bavarian government informing him that his probation had ended and that he was now free to move about without restrictions.

Ah, the irony of it all! mused Franz. *Here I am at the border of Asia, involved in a bitter war. And now the Bavarians are telling me I'm a free man!*

Shaking his head, Franz dropped the letter in the trash.

While the Germans were firmly entrenching themselves in the Caucasus, the Soviets soon rallied their forces and launched a counterattack, pounding their enemies almost daily from the air. Pioneer Company 699, along with the German infantry and artillery, had to be on active duty in order to defend the captured territories. During this terrible time the weaponless Franz remained unscathed while many of his comrades fell.

War often brings out the worst or the best in people, and during the intense fighting an incident demonstrated the kindliness of Hauptmann Miekus. One of the soldiers, a man named Grimm, owned a gold party pin, which indicated that he was a member of the Nazi Party in high standing. He had faithfully served his country throughout the Russian campaign, but now he'd come to the breaking point.

Private Grimm approached a friend one day.

"You know what?" he said. "I've had enough of this hell. I can't take any more. I'm going to smash my gun and desert to the Russian army. Then the war will be over for me. Why don't you come with me?"

Greatly alarmed, the friend reported the conversation to Lieutenant Gutschalk who immediately went to the Hauptmann.

"Hauptmann, I am sorry to report that Private Grimm has talked to the troops about defecting to the Russians, and has urged others to do so. As you know, according to martial law, he must be shot immediately before he can undermine the morale of the company further. I request that he be executed."

The Hauptmann paused in thought. "Lieutenant," he finally said, "send the man to me. I want to talk to him."

Private Grimm was brought to the Hauptmann's quarters, where he remained for over an hour. During roll call that night the Hauptmann addressed the assembled Pioneers who waited tensely for the verdict.

"Soldiers," he said, "in carefully assessing Private Grimm, I have come to the conclusion that he is mentally deranged. His comments cannot be taken seriously." He paused for a moment and gazed around the room, just the faintest twitch of a smile at one corner of his mouth. "It is obvious to me that you are already aware of his condition, since none of you took his suggestion to desert seriously."

The soldiers' tension dissolved in laughter. Grimm went unpunished.

After a few weeks of heavy fighting, the Russians discovered that they couldn't break through the German lines as easily as they thought they could. They retreated hastily, and the Wehrmacht once again continued south. The locals, who were often friendly to the Germans, sabotaged the Russians wherever possible.

The advance followed the usual order. Pioneers Company 699 led the way, repairing or building bridges. The SS followed, routing out and killing as many Jews as they could find. Finally the infantry and artillery arrived and occupied the "cleansed" territories. Again Franz resumed his pattern of going from house to house to warn the Jews.

As they went further south, they came to a region covered with immense fields of sunflowers whose golden faces were turned toward the sun as far as the eye could see. When Company 699 reached the next town, they discovered a large oil mill. Mountains of sunflower seed kernels were piled on the street waiting to be turned into delicious cold pressed sunflower seed oil, the best in the world. Inside, the men discovered gigantic vats filled to the brim with the clear oil. Later they learned that there were 50,000 gallons of oil in storage. The Pioneers were ordered to blow up the mill.

Not wanting to see the oil wasted, Franz came up with a plan and went to speak to the Hauptmann.

"Hauptmann Miekus, I would like to make a suggestion."

"Yes, Hasel?"

"It would be a shame to destroy all that oil. If you would give me permission, Sir, I think I could distribute it fairly among the soldiers. We could fill cans with it and send them home. You know how difficult it is to get any kind of fat in Germany. It would be a great help to our families. Then we can blow up the mill when it is empty."

The Hauptmann squinted skeptically. "I can't imagine how you'll accomplish this feat. But you're right—back home, oil is like gold. If you can pull it off, you have my blessing."

Franz set out to organize the Pioneers into teams. Some collected empty tin cans that had been discarded by the kitchen.

The next group scrubbed the cans until they were sanitary, while others took them to four professional tinsmiths who welded lids back onto each can leaving only a small opening in the top. Then the cans were filled with oil and taken back to the welders, who welded a small tin square over each hole. The cans were distributed among the men who packaged and addressed them and mailed them home.

After the first day, when the operation was running smoothly, Franz took a horse and wagon, filled a 25-gallon barrel with oil, and drove several hours to the field hospital to get more cans. He knew that the wounded at the hospital got nothing but canned goods to eat, so he traded the barrel of oil for a whole wagon full of empty cans.

In the evenings Franz secretly invited the local civilians to pick up oil. They came with water canisters, vodka bottles, and stoneware crocks, and Franz filled them all. Because of this kindness, the grateful population caused the Germans no problems. Within three days Company 699 had emptied the oil vat and dynamited the building.

At home the oil was a godsend. Helene traded some of it for food. She gave one can to the pharmacist, and as a result she was able to get medications that weren't normally available. Another can went to the manager of the apartment building where she lived, and in turn he quickly repaired any damage to her apartment and replaced windows broken by the air pressure during bombing raids.

Again the Pioneers pressed on. The advance, however, slowed down as one tank division after another was pulled out of the Caucasus and sent to assist in the battle of Stalingrad. Finally, at the oil fields of Baku by the Caspian Sea near the Iranian border, the German advance came to a standstill. The battalions remaining in the Caucasus were too decimated to continue.

CHAPTER 13

LIFE IN FRANKFURT

After months in Eschenrod, Helene and the children yearned for the privacy and comforts of their own home.

"Please, Mutti, *please* let's go home," the children begged. "We want to see our cousins and our friends. God can protect us there as well as here!" Finally, Helene gave in. They quickly packed their belongings and piled them high onto the three vehicles they possessed: a battered black bike, the baby buggy, and the stroller.

Early in the morning they set out. This time they couldn't take the train, because large portions of the tracks had been destroyed; they would have to cover the 40 miles on foot.

"Where are you heading?" people along the way asked.

"Frankfurt."

"You'll never make it through," the people said. "All the roads are blocked by tanks."

Helene nodded politely, but inside she was thinking, *Even if 1,000 tanks are blocking the roads, I'm going to get my children home. If the Lord is with us, nothing will happen to us.*

They covered the miles at a steady pace up and downhill. The boys took turns riding the loaded bike, Lotte pushed the stroller, and Helene followed behind with the baby carriage. The going got harder as the day got hotter. Finally, as they started up a long hill, Lotte had no more strength. Helene called to the boys, and Gerd came running.

"Here," he said, when he saw his sister's condition, "give me that." He gripped the stroller's handles in both fists, and with a mighty effort pushed it the rest of the way up the mountain, while Lotte clung to the buggy Helene was pushing. On top they rested.

Helene pointed downward. "Look," she said. "'Way down there I see a house. If we can make it that far, we can get something to eat and drink, and we'll feel better."

Encouraged, the children struggled on. When they reached the house, a woman was leaning out the window calmly watching their approach.

Helene greeted her. "We are on our way to Frankfurt. I have four children. Could you give us something to eat and drink? We'd appreciate it very much."

While they rested in the shade of an apple tree, the woman returned with nothing but a pitcher of water. "Now drink," she said, "and then go. I don't want strays hanging around my place!"

Helene was close to tears. They all took a long drink—and even baby Susi drank the water. Then they continued down the dusty road. As night came, they crawled into an empty hay barn and slept.

Next morning they continued hungry and tired. Soon they were exhausted. The sun burned from the sky, causing perspiration to run like water off their bodies. Helene, whose heart beat as if it were going to burst, had to fight for every breath. Lotte's face was swollen and bluish. Afraid of heat stroke, Helene laid her down by the side of the road in the shade of a wheat field and quietly talked to her, wiping her face with a handful of cool grass.

"Don't be sad," she said. "We'll go just a little farther, and then we will find another house. There'll be shade where we can rest. Be brave, Lotte. God will look after us. Let's continue just a little farther." They got to their feet and labored on in the unbearable heat along the endless miles.

Finally, Lotte called, "Mutti, Mutti, I see a house!"

As they approached, a woman came out. She took one look at them—and Helene cringed inside, waiting for another rebuff. But this woman was different.

"You come with me, inside the gate here," she said, taking hold of the baby buggy. "Rest in the shade while I get you something to eat." Soon she returned with cool peppermint tea, and then a hearty vegetable stew and thick slices of farm bread, which even tiny Susi managed to eat. Soon the little family felt revived and continued on with renewed strength.

That evening, in the distance, they saw the water tower that wasn't far from their home. Helene knew that there was an 8:00 curfew, after which no one was allowed to be on the streets. *We'll never make it in time,* Helene thought. But on they went, and when the armed guards saw the bedraggled lot, they waved them through.

It's still standing, Helene marveled as they turned into their street and saw the apartment building. *Miraculously, it's still standing.* The windows were all blown out again, but no matter. They were home—*home.*

"Mutti," the children begged, "let's stay here and never, never leave again."

"I promise," Helene sighed. For her own sake as well as for the children's, it was a promise she desperately hoped she could keep.

But as fall came and then winter, she began to wonder if she would be able to keep it after all. Food was even scarcer than before. Now, in addition to listing fallen soldiers, the newspapers printed the names of people who had died of starvation. Travel was restricted too. When they wanted to visit Papa's sister Anni and her two children, who lived in downtown Frankfurt, they had to apply for a police pass, which was often denied. Yet they noticed that Nazi members could move about freely.

Food, of course, was top priority. Every night at midnight, Helene woke Kurt. Heavy with sleep, he stumbled out of bed, and with stiff, purple-blue fingers pulled on several layers of clothes, and finally his open-toed shoes. Like the other children, he'd outgrown them—and wouldn't be entitled to another pair until spring—so Helene had cut open the toes to give room for the growing feet.

After gulping down a mug of hot Ersatzkaffee made out of roasted grain, he stepped out of their temporary basement bedroom into the night. Turning his collar up and digging his hands deep into his coat pockets, he bowed his head against the biting wind and walked through the streets to take his place in the bread line. Other isolated figures, dark and lonely, straggled in from other parts of the town. Eventually, they reached their destination—the line in front of the bakery, sometimes 20 people long, sometimes 50, all cold and silent, waiting for their daily ration of bread.

Two hours later a sleepy Gerd arrived to relieve his brother, and Kurt went back home, crawled into bed fully dressed, and hoped that he could get warm enough to go back to sleep. Lotte would then relieve Gerd, and on lucky days the bread would arrive during her turn in line. If there was a delay, Kurt took another turn. Often when the bread-bearer got home, the heel of the loaf was already eaten. Helene didn't have the heart to scold the hungry children.

The stone-cold winter finally gave way to another spring, and as soon as she could, Helene planted spinach in a protected, sunny spot in their garden plot. It soon sprouted. The children knew that it was reserved for the baby who badly needed some enrichment in her diet.

One morning Lotte came home crying from her stint in the bread line. She sat down at the kitchen table still dressed in her threadbare coat. Her wrists were chafed from the cold where her outgrown sleeves no longer covered them.

"What happened?"

"Some of the big kids pushed me out of the line," she sobbed. "I had to go all the way to the back. When I finally got to the bakery, the bread was all gone. And I'm so hungry!"

"We still have a little rice," Helene said comfortingly. "We'll be all right until tomorrow."

Later she went to the garden to get some spinach for Susi, but found that the little patch had been picked clean. In dismay she returned home and demanded an explanation. Kurt confessed to having eaten the spinach. What could Helene do? They were all starving.

One day they had unexpected company. Papa's sister, Tante Anni, and her husband, Onkel Fritz, were at the door. Onkel Fritz was home on furlough. He had been posted to Breslau where he served in the flak artillery, and he told the family that the fighting there was terrible.

"I don't know if I'll make it," he concluded.

They prayed together, and after a few days he went back to his post. It was the last they saw of him. The German forces in Breslau were completely wiped out, with no survivors. Onkel Fritz was listed as missing in action.

Some time later Tante Anni and the cousins, Anneliese and Herbert, again stood at the door. The previous night, while they were in a bunker, their apartment in downtown Frankfurt had been bombed and completely destroyed. For a few days they stayed with the Hasels, and then they were evacuated to a small town on the Rhine River. Would the horror never end?

Helene was assigned a 14 year-old girl to help her with housework. Hitler had decreed that upon leaving elementary school, all girls had to provide a year of free labor as their contribution to the war effort. Thekla was an illegitimate child not wanted at home, and she was glad to be with Helene, who treated her with kindness. However, she had no idea how to take care of a baby and a household, so Helene patiently taught her the necessary tasks. Thekla became very attached to the family, and visited them several times after the war.

As before, the children went to church on Sabbath instead of attending school, making them unpopular with all their instructors. Gerd's math teacher, Herr Neumann, especially took a dislike to his small pupil.

"Hasel," he snapped, "you are defying me. You refuse to use the Hitler greeting, and you stay away on Saturday. But I know how to get the best of you!"

Herr Neumann arranged his lessons so that Saturday was the day on which he would introduce any new math concept. Then, every Monday morning, he pulled his red grade book out of his briefcase, opened it, glanced at the roster of names, and then called on Gerd to come to the board and work the new problems. The first two times, humiliated and frightened, Gerd stood helplessly at the board watching his teacher mark the failing grade, a big "6," in the red book, while his classmates snickered.

Finally he adopted the routine that Kurt and Lotte had been following all along. On Sunday, the three trudged to the houses of their fellow students and asked them what the teachers had covered the day before, and what the homework for Monday was. Since few of his classmates were very interested in math, Gerd usually got three or four different versions. But back home, he took his math book and studied the problems on his own until he mastered the concepts.

The thoroughly unpleasant Herr Neumann had it in for two other boys also, and missed no chance to shame them and mark them down in his hated red book.

"Let's get revenge," they said. So the three of them watched for an opportunity. On the last day of school, they had their chance.

"Herr Neumann's left the grade book lying on his desk!"

Two of the boys acted as lookouts while the third crept into the classroom and snatched it.

"What'll we do with it?"

After a bit of debate, they decided on a ceremonial act of destruction. They divided the tasks and agreed to meet in half an hour on the banks of the river Nidda.

There they set to work. First they flipped through the pages and double-checked the grades. They saw the long row of 6's by their names while other students had scores of 1 and 2.

"That does it," one said. "Is everything ready?"

They placed the book in a battered tin bowl, doused it with gasoline, and set it in the water. Standing back, they lit a match and tossed it into the bowl. As the book burst into flames, someone nudged the bowl with his foot, and they watched gleefully as the current carried the hated red grade book downstream.

Herr Doering, meanwhile, had renewed his campaign of harassment. Soon Helene received another letter from the school. Even before she opened it, she knew what the visit would be about. She explained her situation to the new principal.

"Frau Hasel," he responded, "you and your family are accused of being Jews in disguise. I order you to send your children to school on Saturday!"

Helene had been through this before, and was firm. "My children will not come," she said, "and there is nothing you can do about it. God is able to take care of us."

He slapped his open hand on his desktop. "We'll see about that," he hissed.

Arriving home, Helene told her dismayed children the familiar news.

"Oh, Mutti," Lotte wailed, "the children are already making fun of me. They're so mean. Now it will get even worse."

"Don't be afraid," Helene consoled her. "God has thousands of angels to keep us safe. He can do a miracle."

On Sabbath morning, the family knelt for prayer. Before they got off their knees, the air raid siren sounded.

"Here come the bombers," said Lotte.

Kurt's eyes opened wide. "Why would they fly in the daytime when our Flak can easily shoot them down?" Then he added excitedly, "Mutti, that means no school! School's cancelled during the raids."

Remarkably, from then on to the end of the war, among the incessant nightly air raids over Frankfurt, one happened every Sabbath morning.

Tante Koehler was a faithful Adventist member and one of Helene's friends. Her only son had spoken out against the government and had been arrested and deported to the concentration camp in Dachau. Contrary to policy, she had been given permission to visit him there once and thus was one of the few people who knew about the atrocities committed in the death camps.

She knew a little English, so at night she would secretly place her little radio under the bedcovers and listen to the news on the enemy station, an offense that would have landed her in the death camp if she had been found out.

The German news, of course, was full of propaganda to keep morale as high as possible. "More battles have been won!" the papers shouted. "The Führer makes further advances in the east!" Always, always, Germany was victorious.

But London's BBC told a different story. When Tante Koehler came to visit, she and Helene would whisper behind closed doors. The truth was that the Allies were battering the Germans mercilessly, pushing them back on all fronts.

This can't last much longer, Helene prayed. *Dear God, help it stop. Help it stop.*

By now, even people who didn't listen to the BBC knew that the tide was turning. All they had to do was look at the heavens. Every day, like silver birds high in the sky, enemy planes could be seen flying in formation to unknown destinations. Kurt and Gerd once counted 1,100 planes in one squadron alone.

At night, the same thing always happened. First came the reconnaissance planes, flying high and scouting out the evening's targets, then dropping burning flares that illuminated the area to daylight brightness while they slowly drifted down. Because the markers had a triangular shape, the Germans nicknamed them "Christmas Trees." Then the bombers rumbled over in squadrons of 20, releasing their death-cargo at the same time so the designated areas were carpeted with bombs.

Whenever the evening air raid sirens went off, Helene ran outside to look toward the night sky. Often she saw the dazzling Christmas Trees staking out her own complex of six apartment buildings, probably mistaking them for a German army camp located 20 miles away.

Then she would start to pray.

"Our Father, protect us this night. You are strong and powerful. I know that your angels are surrounding these apartments. Keep us safe."

As she watched, one by one the Christmas Trees went out. By the time the bombers arrived, their target was no longer marked, and they dropped their loads randomly.

Helene and the children huddled in the small basement room, unable to sleep in the inferno and tired to exhaustion. For hours each night they heard the bombs whistling and hissing as they approached the ground, followed by an earth-shattering explosion. If the hit was close by, the whole building shook and the floor rolled like an earthquake. The air pressure shattered the windows and tore open the doors. If someone hadn't made it to the basement in time, they were hurled down the stairs. Shrapnel sprayed through the air. The bombardments were endless. The constant danger, the lack of sleep, and the cold tore at everyone's nerves. But throughout the entire war, not one bomb scored a direct hit on those six apartment buildings.

After extra heavy attacks, Kurt and Gerd took the family's wooden handcart and pulled it the five miles into the city center. They had to pick their way carefully through the rubble that littered the streets. Often there were charred bodies shrunk to a third of their normal size—the remains of people who had fled their houses during a raid and had been burned by phosphorous bombs.

The buildings were still smoldering after the raging fires. Carefully, the boys pulled out beams, doors, window frames, anything else that could burn. Sometimes they found unexploded mines, which they laid aside and continued on their way. They didn't fully comprehend the danger of these devices until one of Kurt's schoolmates got his hand blown off when he handled a grenade. When their cart was loaded, they hauled their take home for Helene to use in heating and cooking.

A favorite pastime of the boys became searching the ground for pieces of unusually shaped shrapnel. These were highly prized among the children and could be used to barter for other treasures.

Herr Doering continued to plot Helene's downfall. He hatched up a new scheme: Kurt, almost 14, was ordered to join the Jungvolk, Hitler's organization for boys between 10 and 14. These young people learned survival skills, went to social functions, sang patriotic songs, and participated in vigorous physical exercises.

Maybe this is a way my son can participate without violating his principles, Helene thought. *It sounds harmless and benevolent. Why antagonize the Nazis when we don't have to?*

Kurt obeyed the summons and went to the enlistment office. After he'd filled out the paperwork he was issued the regulation Jungvolk uniform: tan trousers, a brown four-button shirt with a turned-down collar and two patch breast pockets, a brown cloth peaked cap, a black neckerchief gathered at the throat by a brown leather ring, and a black leather belt—its shiny buckle imprinted with the German eagle clutching the swastika and circled by the bold legend "Blood and Honor."

As he listened to the chatter swirling around him, however, Kurt began to wonder how harmless this venture was going to be. Strutting proudly in their uniforms, the other boys bragged about future power positions, and how being promoted into the Hitler Youth was the sure route to make it into the esteemed ranks of the SS, Hitler's elite forces. Maybe this wasn't a suitable organization for a young Christian after all.

Immediately Kurt was assigned to Sabbath duty. Quietly he made the decision to stay home. There were so many kids that maybe they wouldn't notice his absence. He was mistaken.

The Hitler Youth leader, himself an immature youth of 17, came to the Hasel apartment early one morning.

"Frau Hasel," he said in an insolent tone when she opened the door, "Kurt plays hooky from civic duty on Saturdays. I am here to demand that he report this Saturday!"

Helene eyed him calmly. "You cannot tell me what to do," she said. "You're only a little older than Kurt yourself. I am his mother, and I'm the one who determines where he goes, not you."

The young leader had evidently been watching his superiors, because he behaved exactly as they did. He stiffened.

"I'll show *you* who is in charge here," he barked. "I'll report you to the party. Then we'll see who is boss!"

"You do what you have to do." And Helene closed the door on him.

Next time he saw Kurt, the leader hissed, "I'd like to kick you so hard you couldn't walk any more. You think you're so high and mighty. I'll fix you!"

The response from the party was immediate. Kurt received a hand–delivered letter. He was being drafted into the army for immediate posting to the front. He was to report to duty that afternoon at 4:00.

When Helene read the notice, she had the impression that someone was tapping her on the shoulder. When she spun around, no one was there. She thought she heard a voice whispering, "Hurry, hurry! Why are you hesitating?" The voice increased in urgency.

Suddenly Helene knew what she had to do.

"Kurt," she said. "Get your bike and ride to Eschenrod. Here is a little piece of bread. Put it in your pocket."

"Can't I take some more food in my backpack?"

Helene shook her head. "You can't take anything along. Otherwise the neighbors will know you are escaping."

Kurt took a deep breath and shook his head in bewilderment at these rapid decisions. "What about you? They'll come for you."

"I will follow with the children. Gerd?"

"Here, Mutti."

"Gerd, go outside and see if anyone is watching."

When all was clear, Kurt set out and quickly disappeared from sight.

Helene ran through the apartment gathering up a few of the most necessary items. With these she carefully padded the baby carriage. She could not take much. It must look as if they were just taking the baby on her customary afternoon walk. She put Susi in the buggy and gathered Gerd and Lotte around her

"Stay right here for a minute," she said, and stepped across the landing to a trusted neighbor's door. She knocked softly.

The door opened a crack, then wider, and the woman pulled her inside.

"I have come to say good-bye again," Helene began. "We are going to the country. I can't tell you where."

The woman winked, "I understand. You just go in peace. If anyone asks me, I know of nothing. I'll keep an eye out for your husband."

Gratefully Helene shook her hand. Then she and the children stepped outside. No one saw them leave.

Later Helene learned from her neighbor what had happened that afternoon. By 5:00 the Hitler Youth leader accompanied Herr Doering and another party official to the apartment. They found only a closed door. They rang the bell, knocked, and kicked the door. They looked into the windows and saw that nobody was there.

"Just you wait!" they shouted in frustration. "We'll get you. We'll come back and get you out of bed, you draft dodger! Then you will finally get what you deserve!"

They rang the neighbor's doorbell.

"Is Frau Hasel home?"

"I'm sorry," she said truthfully, "I don't know where she is. Have you tried ringing her bell?"

"We'll be back tonight and get Kurt—if we have to force the door."

With a shrug, the woman went back inside.

At midnight they returned. They hammered on the Hasels' door for a while, and again they rang the neighbor's bell. She was ready for them.

"I have had enough of this!" she screamed. "It's the middle of the night. Get out of here and leave me in peace!" She slammed her door and double-locked it. The men banged on the doors of other apartments, but nobody opened. Enraged, they finally left.

All this time Helene and the children plodded along the familiar road. The miles stretched endlessly. Russian prisoners-of-war were trudging in the same direction, living skeletons, their bloody feet wrapped in rags. When Helene stopped to give the children a slice of bread, they watched with burning, hollow eyes. Helene took her own piece and gave half to one of the men. He greedily devoured it.

As they walked along, one of the Russians, a young man, looked into the buggy. When he saw Susi, he gently stroked her little cheek. Then for miles he walked beside the carriage holding the baby's hand, tears streaming down his emaciated face and falling in the dust of the road. Helene's heart went out to him. She wondered if he had a baby of his own at home.

Dusty and starving, they arrived in Eschenrod two days later. The Josts, never expecting to see them again, had taken other evacuees into their home. But Herr Straub, the mayor of the village, agreed to give them shelter. As they fell into bed, they wondered what would await them here.

CHAPTER 14

BIBLE STUDIES

While his family struggled in Frankfurt, Franz had contracted malaria. After months of illness, he slowly recuperated. One day he was told to go to the Hauptmann.

As usual, Franz saluted with his hand to his head. "You wanted to see me, sir?"

"Hasel, you have been ill, and you have not had a leave for a long time. You are entitled to a furlough. If you leave right away, you could be home by Christmas. Be back in three weeks. Good luck! Safe travels!" Miekus held out his hand, and Franz shook it warmly.

Is it possible? Wondered Franz. *Can I really be home for Christmas? Will I find my family? Do I still have a home?*

He packed in haste, filling his bags with cans of oil, bread, butter, canned goods, and local cheese he bought from the peasants. Then he set out. No systematic travel plans could be made. Trains went where the tracks were intact—and that changed from day to day.

He boarded a freight train and headed in the direction of Poland. Finally they reached the border at Brest-Litovsk. From there he boarded a train that was to take him west across Poland to Germany.

No sooner had Franz found a seat and the train started rolling when there was a commotion outside. Whistles blew. SS men ran down the length of the platform shouting for the engineer to stop.

"What's going on?" Franz inquired of a soldier.

"They forgot to put an empty car in front of the engine."

Franz looked uncomprehending. "Why do we need an empty car?"

"Where have you been? Don't you know that the Polish partisans lay explosives on the tracks? If we hit one of those spots, only the empty car will be blown up, not the whole train."

No, Franz did not know that. In the Caucasus the relations between the Wehrmacht and the civilians was friendly and cordial. There had been no sabotage.

The journey continued. Sometimes the train had to take a detour because the tracks were damaged. Other times it stood on a siding for hours while bombs hailed down. Through it all, on Christmas morning they arrived safely in Frankfurt. How terrible the city looked! Bombs had destroyed nearly half of it. The streets were covered by rubble and smoldering cinder.

Franz hurried home wondering what he would find. In the distance he could already see the apartment buildings. They still stood! As he approached the door, Helene tore it open and fell into his arms. She had recognized him by his gait.

"Children, children, come quickly! Papa is home!"

What a Christmas celebration they had! With the food that Franz brought, Helene prepared a feast. They had not heard from each other in many months. And now they were all together again safe and sound. There was so much to share. In the evening, tired and happy, they had a service of praise and thanksgiving.

The next day Franz went to visit church members. As he left, he warned his children to leave his things alone. But the temptation was too great for Gerd. He sneaked into the bedroom and explored his father's gear. He put on Franz's side hat, strapped on his holster, and strutted around pretending to be a big powerful soldier. Suddenly his father stood before him, his face as white as chalk. He shut the door and turned to his little boy.

"Gerd, what have you done? Didn't I tell you to stay away from my things?"

"Papa, I just . . . I only . . . I didn't hurt anything, I promise!"

"Gerd, come here. You discovered something that no one else in the world knows. Did you notice that I have a piece of wood in my holster instead of a revolver? I carry this so that Satan cannot tempt me to kill someone and break God's commandments. But it is treason and a crime to be a soldier without a weapon. If anyone finds out, they will shoot me, and you won't have a Papa anymore. You must promise me not to tell anyone."

Frightened and sobbing Gerd stammered, "I promise, Papa! I didn't know! I don't want you to get killed! I won't ever tell anyone!"

"Go then and play. Forget what you saw here!"

Little Gerd felt the weight of carrying such a big responsibility. Of course he would never give his Papa away. It was, however, a wonderful opportunity to prove his importance to his older brother and sister. He couldn't pass up the chance. When he found them he chanted, "I know something that you don't know! It's a big secret between Papa and me, and nobody but us two can know about it! If I tell, he will get killed!"

With that he pranced away, leaving the other two dying with curiosity and mad because they had not been let into the secret. When Gerd decided to have a better look at the wooden "pistol," he found the bedroom door locked.

All too soon the visit came to an end, and Franz had headed back to Russia. Travel conditions by then were such that it took him a whole three months to rejoin his unit. On the way he met up with his two old friends, Willi and Karl.

At one point in that three-month journey, the men found a large radio. Knowing that if they were caught listening to enemy stations they'd be punished, they still turned the radio dial trying to find war news. London's BBC told of Russian advances and German defeats, while the German station aired a rousing speech by Goebbels stating that Germany was mobilizing 50 new divisions at home and was ready to launch a total offensive that would be the beginning of the final victory.

Franz and his friends looked at each other and slowly shook their heads.

"That's absurd," Karl whispered. "Where on earth is Germany going to find enough men to set up 50 new divisions?"

Finally they reached Dzankoj in the Crimea. Walking down the street, Willi suddenly pointed across to the other side.

"My, my," he murmured. "Look who's over there!"

The other men turned their heads to see Lieutenant "Seldomcheerful" Gutschalk striding purposefully along.

The three crossed the street, saluted, and reported back to duty. The lieutenant, who had arrived that day to consult with an army dentist, reluctantly asked them to join him in his room for the night. Company 699 was stationed in Simferopol, a day's journey away, and the men would have to wait until tomorrow to rejoin it.

When they reached the lieutenant's quarters, they discovered a single brass bed. Naturally the senior officer was entitled to it, so the others lay on the floor. Half an hour later, a cursing Peter Gutschalk jumped out of bed.

"What's the matter, Lieutenant?"

"I can't stand it! The bed is swarming with bed bugs, and they're eating me alive!"

When the men turned on the light, hundreds of bedbugs fled up the walls and disappeared while the unlucky lieutenant scratched the welts they had left on his body. He joined the others on the floor—where they hadn't been bothered at all.

The next day Franz, Willi, and Karl reunited with Pioneer Park Company 699 in the Crimea. Franz found his office intact and even his remaining private possessions undisturbed. He resumed his old duties.

One warm Wednesday Franz sat on the wooden bench outside his quarters. He had just finished his lunch and was enjoying a few minutes in the sun. As was his habit when he took a break, he was reading his Bible. Just then, Lieutenant Gutschalk walked by. The very sight of Franz made his hackles rise.

"Hasel, I see you are reading your book of Jewish fairy tales again. I cannot understand how an enlightened person can believe that garbage. You are nothing but a disguised Jew and a communist. If I had my way, you would be liquidated like them."

Just in time Franz remembered the text in Amos: "Therefore the prudent man keeps quiet in such times, for the times are evil!"

He let the insult go unchallenged.

Franz's silence enraged Gutschalk even more. His veins stood out on his neck like cords as he raged, "I am watching you. One day you are going to slip up, and then I will destroy you!"

A few days later Hauptmann Miekus sauntered into the office and closed the door behind him.

"So Hasel," he said, "you know a lot about the Bible, don't you?"

"I know some things," Franz responded cautiously.

"Come with your Bible to my quarters tomorrow morning at 8:00. I have some questions I want to ask you."

"Yes, sir!" Franz said. *What's he getting at?* he wondered. *What new trial am I in for now?*

Punctually the next morning Franz entered the Hauptmann's room. To his surprise, Sergeant Erich and Lieutenant Gutschalk were also present. Miekus motioned Franz to the remaining chair at the table.

Without delay the Hauptmann asked, "Somewhere in the Bible it says something about being punished to the third and fourth generation. What is that all about?"

"That's part of the Ten Commandments." Franz turned to Exodus 20 and read to them.

"I remember from my childhood that it talks about a lake of fire."

"Yes, that's in Revelation 20, where it talks about the final judgment." Franz found the passage and explained its meaning.

Finally the Hauptmann's eyebrows twitched in admiration. "So you do know your Bible inside and out."

Franz's eyes twinkled. He pinched his Bible between thumb and forefinger and held it up. "I know the outside," he said. "It's black leather. And I also know the inside a little bit."

He glanced around at the rest of them, and since no one jumped into the conversation, he decided to take the lead.

"Hauptmann Miekus," he began, "I understand that in civilian life you are a history professor."

"That's right."

"I wonder if you could help me."

The Hauptmann inclined his head graciously. "I will do my best."

"The Bible contains some prophecies with historical content that were written around 600 BC," Franz said. "And I have always wanted to check them out with an expert in the field. Would you be willing to let me present them, and then give me your feedback on the accuracy of the facts?"

Flattered, the unsuspecting Hauptmann responded, "I'd be glad to. Go right ahead."

Franz now pulled out the worn postcard that he had carried in his wallet since 1921 when he had been baptized as a convert from Catholicism. On the card's front was a picture of the image described in Daniel 2, and on the back Franz had carefully typed the dates and events corresponding to each part of the image.

He carefully went through the chapter verse by verse discussing the empires of Babylon, Medo-Persia, Greece, and Rome. After three and a half hours he turned to the Hauptmann.

"Do I have everything correct?" he asked. "As I say, I'm no expert in history. I'd be grateful to you if you would point out any errors."

"No," the astonished officer replied. "No errors. Everything is accurate." He gazed at the sergeant and the lieutenant, then back to Franz. "Hasel, I have never heard anything so amazing in my life."

"You see what a timely book the Bible is, sir." Franz paused for effect. "Yet can you imagine," he continued, "that there are still individuals in the Third Reich who say that people who read the Bible are disguised Jews and communists and ought to be liquidated?"

The Hauptmann's brows lowered in a puzzled frown. "What's that? Do people really say that?"

"Yes, Herr Hauptmann!" Franz allowed his gaze to rest just for a moment on Peter Gutschalk's ears. They were bright red, and the lieutenant seemed not to know where to look in his embarrassment.

"Well, Franz," said Hauptmann Miekus. "Back to the book. You haven't finished. We got as far as the iron legs of Rome. What do the feet represent?"

Franz explained the 10 toes representing the 10 tribes of modern Europe. He described the characteristics of iron and clay that make it impossible for these two substances to stick together. With that, he brought the Bible study to a conclusion.

The Hauptmann was quiet for a moment. "Well?" he finally asked. "What does it mean?"

Franz took a careful breath, and prayed for courage as he did so.

"Herr Hauptmann," he said, "the only conclusion a Bible student can come to is that the Führer cannot win this war. It will not be possible for him to unite Europe under his leadership and establish his 1,000-year Third Reich."

He looked earnestly into the Hauptmann's face. "Sir, the Bible's predictions have been proved accurate again and again. And if they're accurate here, it means that we're fighting a losing battle."

Dead silence.

Finally, the Hauptmann glanced at his watch. "It's noon! We need to hurry otherwise we'll get nothing to eat! Where has the time gone?"

He stood up, and the others instantly rose in respect.

"Hasel."

"Yes, Herr Hauptmann?"

"May I borrow your Bible for a few days?"

"Certainly, sir. I have another copy in my room. Here, just let me remove my notes. Keep it as long as you like."

In a daze the men left the Hauptmann's quarters. Lieutenant Gutschalk carefully avoided eye contact with Franz.

A week later the Hauptmann returned the Bible.

"Hasel," he said, "I appreciate what you shared with me." He looked around, and lowered his voice. "From now on we will no longer operate a third of our motorized vehicles. The gasoline rations thus saved I want you to store in drums and canisters so that when the end comes we will have enough fuel to get back home."

"Yes, sir."

"And remember, Hasel. This is just between you and me."

CHAPTER 15

THE AMERICANS ARRIVE

Helene was torn out of sleep by gunfire and screaming. With pounding heart she listened to the sounds in the early dawn. Through six years of war she had struggled to keep herself and her four children alive. Now the end had come.

The Russians are here, she thought in horror. *And there's no place to hide in our apartment. Only God can help us now.*

Lying paralyzed with fear, she listened to the increasing commotion outside.

Wait. Those aren't Russian sounds. Those men are speaking the dialect of Upper Hessen farmers. Why are they in Frankfurt?

Suddenly it all came back. She and the children had made their escape from Frankfurt and had arrived in Eschenrod late the previous night.

Then what was the noise? There had been no news that the Russians were close. Now fully awake, she slipped out of bed, padded barefoot across the rough floorboards to the window, and looked out.

The farmyard was filled with men. Their attention was focused on a mud-covered pig that was desperately trying to break through their circle. Again and again as the men lunged for it, the slippery pig slid through their hands. Herr Straub, their landlord, shot his rifle into the air adding to the confusion.

Suddenly Kurt, Lotte, and Gerd crowded her at the window.

"What are they doing to the pig, Mutti?" asked Lotte.

"They are going to slaughter it."

"But the pig is afraid. Just listen to how it squeals. How can they do that?"

Helene put a comforting arm around her. "Lotte, this is how you get meat. You know how we sometimes eat beef. It comes from cows that are slaughtered."

The men had now caught the pig and wrestled it to the ground. Herr Straub drove a dagger into its neck, and a fountain of blood mingled with the mud. Eleven-year-old Lotte jerked away from the window and threw herself on the bed, sobbing and retching.

"I'm never, ever going to eat meat again," she wept.

Helene got dressed, then picked baby Susi up and changed her diapers on the bed while the others took turns washing themselves in the icy water that had been sitting in the pitcher on the wash stand all night.

Downstairs in the farm kitchen, Frau Straub had already baked several loaves of bread. She invited Helene and the children to join them for a breakfast of buttered bread and Ersatzkaffee.

"What are the conditions in your city?" Herr Straub asked her.

"Most of Frankfurt is in ruins," Helene said. "Every night there is a hail of bombs as squadrons of enemy planes systematically cover the city."

"It's good that you came here," Herr Straub said kindly. "You will be safe with us. Frankfurt is no place for children at a time like this."

He reached for his battered gray felt hat and went outside to cut up the pig. Soon sides of bacon were hanging in the smokehouse to cure, and Frau Straub was boiling sausages in the big kettles usually used for doing the laundry.

Helene and the children, sickened by the smell of cooking pork, returned upstairs to the room the Straubs had assigned to them. Quickly they made the three beds. Then 14-year-old Kurt got the Bible and read the story of God's protection of faithful Joseph. Helene led the family in prayer.

"Thank You, Lord," she prayed, "for once again protecting us and bringing us safely to this haven deep in the Vogelsberg mountains. No one at home saw us leave, and no one knows where we are. Please, God, let us have some peace here. And please watch over our Papa. It has been months since we last heard from him. He was in Russia then. You know where he is now, and You can guard him there as well as You're guarding us here."

The children fervently echoed her "Amen."

They spent the whole morning placing the household items they had brought in the old dresser in their room, and hanging up their clothes in the ancient carved wardrobe whose worm-eaten doors were decorated with painted roses. When everything was stowed, Helene closed its creaking doors and turned the heavy ornate key.

Then she went to the kitchen where Lotte was already busy peeling potatoes and scraping carrots for a simple vegetable soup. Later, while Susi took her nap, the other three children went outside to explore.

Soon Kurt rushed back into the house, ashen faced.

"Kurt, Kurt, what happened?" Helene cried. "What's the matter?"

Unable to speak, he held out a dripping object. She took it out of his shaking hands and spread it on the kitchen table. It was a poster demanding that youth who had escaped from being drafted into the army were to report immediately to the recruiting office. Any young draft-dodgers caught in hiding would immediately be shot to death.

"Kurt." Helene's voice shook. "Where did this come from?"

"I saw a Nazi official nailing it on the village announcement board. After he left, the wind tore the poster off and blew it into the creek. I was curious what it said, so I fished it out with a long stick. Oh Mutti, what shall we do?"

"We must tell the mayor," she said resolutely. "He has been kind in taking us in. But if he is discovered harboring a fugitive, he will be executed. We can't do this to him."

Helene went into the yard where the butchering continued.

"Herr Straub," she said in a low voice. "Could you come into the house for a moment?"

Seeing her obvious distress, he followed her into the kitchen wiping his bloody hands on his pants.

"Is something wrong, Frau Hasel?" he asked.

Helene explained Kurt's find. Silently the mayor read the poster spread out on the table. Then he crumpled it up and threw it onto the glowing coals in the stove.

Helene whispered, "Herr Straub, I have to confess something to you. We came here because Kurt was summoned for the draft. We cannot put you into such danger. Oh, what shall we do?"

"Frau Hasel," the mayor said quietly, "the wind tore a poster off and blew it into the creek. I saw nothing and know nothing about it."

He sauntered over to the window, looked out, and returned to her side. "I have a confession to make too," he told her soberly.

"I have secretly been listening to the BBC's German-language broadcasts from London. As you know, it is forbidden to listen to the enemy station, and if I am found out, I will be arrested. But these, Frau Hasel, are desperate times that call for desperate behavior. I have learned that the Germans are broadcasting nothing but lies. We are not winning the war. In fact, the war will soon be over. The Americans are very close to Eschenrod, and will be here soon. And we are not sending your boy into the fighting lines at this late stage. Thousands of untrained children like him are being slaughtered daily"—he gestured toward the window— "just like that pig out there. This is madness. You must keep Kurt hidden in the house, because we are not going to sacrifice him now."

Helene pressed Herr Straub's hand. It was impossible for her to speak.

Two weeks later rumors circulated that the Americans were approaching. A steady stream of retreating German soldiers came through Eschenrod. Kurt stepped outside to watch the ragged troops of his defeated country file by. The captain of one unit spotted him.

"Boy. Come here."

"Yes, sir?"

"I have several boxes of classified documents here," said the officer. "We can't transport them any longer. I order you to burn them. Show me to the village oven."

Kurt took him to the large brick oven where all the peasants baked their bread. The captain ordered his soldiers to carry the boxes there. They dumped them on the ground, then hurried after their disappearing comrades while Kurt began tossing the papers into the flames. For several hours he burned sheaf after sheaf of documents till the oven was red-hot and clouds of ashes flew out of the chimney. The raging fire consumed documents marked "Secret" and "Top Secret" in which Hitler himself had given orders that directed the fighting on the Maginot Line.

In the early afternoon Herr Straub shot into the kitchen.

"The Americans are within five miles!" he cried. "They'll be here in a couple of hours. Oh, what am I supposed to do?"

Thinking fast, Helene tried to calm him. "Why don't you send messengers to each house and tell the people to hang white sheets out of their windows?" she suggested. "That will signal to them that we're surrendering."

Grateful for the recommendation, Herr Straub did as she said, and soon white bedsheets billowed from every window as the first American trucks rumbled into the village. It was Good Friday 1945.

"Attention! Attention!" the loudspeakers on their trucks crackled in German. "Anyone leaving their houses will be shot. Remain in your houses."

Soon soldiers were banging on each door. Helene opened the Straub's door, and 35 men crowded into the house. They were very friendly, went into the kitchen, and started pulling out pots and pans. Using sign language they asked for bread and fat to fry some eggs.

Helene searched out the terrified Frau Straub, who was hiding in the attic.

"Look, the men are hungry," she reasoned with her. "Don't let them wait so long. Give them some food. That's all they want."

"They are going to eat up all my stores," Frau Straub lamented. "But if it has to be this way, give them a lump of lard and a loaf of bread."

Helene shook her head. "That will never do," she insisted. "Don't be foolish. Give them enough to eat; otherwise they will take everything. Your life is more important than a pot of lard."

Finally, Frau Straub said, "Frau Hasel, you take over. Do what you think is right."

Helene rushed into the cellar and got butter, eggs, crusty loaves of bread, pitchers of the home brewed hard cider, and the blue earthenware crock of lard. Then she stoked the fire and started frying eggs. The leader of the GI's knew a few words of German and asked Helene for this and that. She quickly brought what was needed.

While she was standing over the hot stove, one of the men came up behind her, put his arm around her, and started to kiss her. In a flash the commander was at her side. He loudly scolded the soldier and knocked him into a corner. After that, nobody dared bother her again.

That night as a dead-tired Helene went up the dark stairs to her room, someone tugged on her sleeve.

She jumped in fright. "Who is it?"

A female voice whispered, "Frau Hasel, please let me hide in your room. I don't feel safe by myself."

It was Frau Haar, another Frankfurt woman who had found refuge with the Straubs. She had been in great danger at home because she had helped a Russian prisoner-of-war to escape. Word of this got around the neighborhood, and she had to flee to avoid being arrested and sent to a concentration camp.

Without a word, Helene took her by the hand and led her into the room. Susi was already asleep in her crib, and the other children got ready for bed. Kurt and 9-year old Gerd shared one bed, Lotte had another, and Helene and Frau Haar decided to share the double bed. Before the children climbed into their beds, Helene knelt with them and prayed for protection in the night.

"Frau Haar," she said after the children were tucked in, "we don't know what this night will bring. We'd better not get undressed. That way we can be ready at a moment's notice."

Suddenly a timid knock sounded on the door. Helene opened the door a crack and saw the 12-year old orphan girl the Straubs had hired to herd their cows.

"Frau Hasel, I am so scared. Please let me stay in your room," the shivering girl begged. Helene pulled her in and locked the door again.

"You can share the bed with Lotte," she said, and tucked the girl in. Soon all was quiet and Helene fell asleep. At 2:00 a.m. she was awakened by shouting, screaming, and raucous laughter. Footsteps were coming up the stairs. Immediately, she heard Frau Straub's voice outside the door.

"Frau Hasel, open up quickly! The Americans want to inspect your room!"

Helene jumped out of bed thinking, "Now I and Frau Haar are done for." The soldiers had already stumbled up the stairs, reeking of alcohol.

Opening the door, she saw standing there the troop leader who had protected her earlier in the kitchen.

"Oh," he said in simple German. "You here."

He shone his flashlight into the corners of the room and under the beds. Then he carefully played it over each bed. Other men wanted to push past him, but he stood broad legged in the doorway yelling at the others, "Get out! Get out!"

He turned to Helene and asked, "Your children?" Silently Helene nodded her head. He said, "You good woman. You sleep." He turned and motioned for her to lock the door behind him.

Sabbath morning, when Helene went down to the kitchen to heat some milk for breakfast, she found several village women gathered there.

"How did you get through the night, Frau Hasel?" they wanted to know.

"I had no problems. I slept."

"What, the soldiers didn't molest you?"

To her horror, Helene learned that the drunken men had raped the women of the village, from little girls to grandmothers. None had been spared. Sobbing, the women sat around the table recounting the terrors of the night.

Helene also heard stories of farmers who pretended they had nothing left when soldiers came to ask for food. The enraged GI's went to the cellars where the food stores were kept and hacked to pieces everything they found.

One family's daughter was going to be confirmed in the church the following Sunday. For months they had been hoarding food for the feast and hid it behind some fake paneling in the living room. The soldiers, knocking with their guns on the walls, discovered the hollow place, kicked in the paneling and found bacon, ham, butter, eggs, and a big pot filled to the top with golden honey.

Infuriated that they had been lied to, the men threw everything on the floor and trampled on it till all was ruined. They saved the honey pot till last. Finally one of the men grabbed it and defecated in it.

"We even had to throw the pot away," the disconsolate woman reported.

Later that day the American commander gave orders that on penalty of death no women were to be molested. But the damage had been done. Only the women around Helene had been spared.

After breakfast Helene gathered the children around her and conducted Sabbath School. They sang their favorite song: "A mighty fortress is our God, a bulwark never failing."

The village streets were deserted, but no more violence occurred that day or the following night, which the terrified villagers spent behind bolted doors and shuttered windows.

Life settled into a routine under the occupation forces. The Americans ruled with a light hand, and became ruthless only when faced with what they considered treason. . . .

In a village near Eschenrod lived a farmer who had four sons. He had lost three of them in the war, and the one still alive was a member of Hitler's elite SS troops. Like all SS men, he had sworn an oath of loyalty to Hitler and felt he couldn't betray that and surrender to the enemy. When the Americans discovered him, they took him into a field and shot him, then cut his head off with a spade. Village children found his mutilated body, and he was brought back to his parents on an oxcart covered with straw. Heartbroken, the grieving parents buried their last son.

In Eschenrod, Kurt, Gerd, and Lotte enjoyed watching the soldiers. They were good-natured and jolly and liked children, and sometimes gave them candy. One day the first black men the children had ever seen joined the other GI's, and the children watched them in fascination, wondering if the black skin color might be shoe polish.

Always daring, Gerd decided it was time to do a bit of hands-on scientific investigation. He walked up to one of the black soldiers and held out his hand for a handshake. When he pulled it back, he carefully inspected his palm to see if any of the color had come off. The GI, noticing his curiosity, chuckled and encouraged him to touch his skin. Gerd rubbed and rubbed on his arm, but it stayed black.

Satisfied that it was genuine, Gerd gave the man a big grin. The soldier pulled out a pack of Juicy Fruit gum, and Gerd grabbed it eagerly, but then didn't know what to do with it. The man pantomimed chewing on it, and when Gerd tried a piece he suddenly discovered why the Americans were forever chewing.

Spring came and with it the Allied offensive intensified. At night, Mutti and Kurt watched the orange sky as many miles away Frankfurt was burning. Then one day they heard that Eschersheim, their own suburb, had been completely destroyed.

"Kurt," Mutti said. "I won't have any peace until I know the truth about this. Why don't you take Papa's bicycle and go to Frankfurt and see if anything remains of our apartment?"

"Sure," Kurt said, always ready for adventure. "If the apartment's gone, I'll find someone to stay with overnight."

"I'm going to give you some butter and flour for the apartment manager. And I'll wait for you tomorrow at the edge of the forest with bread and peppermint tea because I know you'll be hungry. Hurry now. And don't linger anywhere because the forests are dangerous."

As Kurt reached an area of open fields, he suddenly heard the drone of approaching bombers high overhead. Bombs began exploding around him, and he toppled off his bicycle and lay flat. The planes had evidently been aiming for the railway station in nearby Gedern but had missed their target.

Once the thunderous blasts ceased, he mounted his bicycle and struggled on. Then low-flying planes approached and started shooting at him. He threw himself into a ditch and hid his head in his arms, praying to God for protection. When all was quiet again, he continued on his way.

After several hours, he saw in the distance Eschersheim's water tower, the landmark that was close to his apartment building. As he rode closer, he was amazed to see that amid the smoldering ruins, their apartment complex of six buildings still stood tall against the sky.

He unlocked the apartment door and went inside. It was dark. The concussion of the bombs had blown the window glass out, and Herr Georg, the manager, had nailed heavy cardboard to the frames. Kurt gave him the items he had brought from Eschenrod, and he and his wife—who had tuberculosis—gratefully accepted the much-needed food.

The next morning Kurt left the sad sights behind and once again headed into the country. It was hot, and he grew weak from hunger, but finally the Eschenrod forest appeared, and he saw Mutti waiting in the shade as she had promised.

As he came around the last bend toward her, a Pole jumped out of the bushes, grabbed Kurt's handlebars and forced him off the bike. He shoved Kurt to the side, mounted the bike, and rode off.

Mutti had seen what had happened. Just then a line of American tanks rounded the curve behind her. She darted into the road and stood in their path with outstretched arms. They stopped, but nobody could understand German, and after a few frustrating minutes they continued on their way. Mutti and Kurt walked to the village and hurried to the schoolhouse where the Americans were stationed.

"Does anyone here speak German?" Mutti demanded.

A young blond soldier who had been whittling on a piece of wood while sitting on his cot stepped forward and asked in perfect German, "What do you want?"

"We need help. A Pole just stole my husband's bike from us."

"Well, where's your husband?"

"My husband is in Russia."

As they chatted Mutti asked him how an American could speak German so well.

"My mother came from a village not far from here," he said. "She was very homesick and longed to come back, but my father showed no understanding. So when I was a little boy, she held me on her lap and taught me German Christmas songs. She said to me, 'Jim, we celebrate Christmas by giving presents, but we also remember God. Never forget that Jesus came into the world for us.' She had such a good heart, but my father never allowed her to visit her homeland, and she died of a broken heart. Her last words to me were, 'Jim, find my village. Find my father's house. There are beautiful flowers in the windows'. Now I hope to visit there."

Jim smiled at Mutti. "Don't worry. If you can describe that bike carefully, we'll find it and get it back for you. Come next Wednesday morning. I'll leave it in the basement of that house across the road there." He pointed across the street. Mutti recognized the house; a former Adventist had moved there not too long ago.

On Wednesday Mutti went to the house and knocked on the door.

"No bike here," said the woman emphatically when Mutti asked her about it.

Discouraged, Mutti turned away. But a moment later she noticed the landlord—who'd heard everything—motioning to her.

"She's lying," he whispered. "That bike was delivered. The soldier told me to keep an eye out for you, so I did some checking. She's locked it in the cellar and covered it with blankets."

Mutti crossed the street to the schoolhouse, found Jim, and told him what had happened.

Jim's face hardened. "We'll see about that," he said, straightening his cap. They crossed the street together, and Jim knocked at the woman's door.

"I brought a bike here yesterday," he said. "Produce it."

"I know nothing about it," the woman said blandly.

"You either produce that bike," said Jim in his best SS-trooper voice, "or I'll arrest you."

The woman's lips tightened, but her eyes lowered. Wordlessly she led them to her cellar and gave them the bicycle.

Oh, Mutti thought to herself as she wheeled it away. *Oh, if the war could end as easily! What was to become of them all? Was her husband still alive?*

Early one Sunday the rumble of tanks rolling through the streets roused the frightened population. Kurt, his eye glued to a chink in the shutter, whispered, "They are lining up by the bridge. Now soldiers are moving into position on the other side."

Suddenly they heard a heavily accented voice announcing from a bullhorn mounted on an army jeep: *"Achtung! Achtung!* All women and children must immediately assemble on the village bridge! This is an order!" As the jeep disappeared, the order was repeated again and again, its echoes bouncing off the walls of the houses.

Frightened, Gerd clung to his mother's hand. Lotte, white as a sheet, asked, "Mutti, must we go? What is going to happen to us?"

Helene made a quick decision. "Kurt, I want you to go to the attic and hide. Make sure no one sees you. It looks like something bad is going to happen, and we may not come back. If our Papa returns from the war, someone must be able to tell him what happened to us. Quick, now!"

While Kurt ran up the creaking attic stairs, Helene quickly wrapped the other three in sweaters and shawls, all the while praying silently for protection. Then taking Susi on her arm, and instructing the other two to hold on to her skirts, she hurried to the bridge. It was already crowded with women and children, and their anxious whispers sounded around her: "What happened? What is going on? What does this mean?"

Helene suddenly felt a peace descend on her. In her mind's eye she could see angels guarding them.

Up in the attic, Kurt found a knothole through which he could command a view of the village square. He saw the women and children on the bridge. They were surrounded by Americans—on one side the soldiers with their machine guns trained on the bridge; on the other side tanks with their guns pointed at the women. There was no way of escape.

Kurt saw the set lines in the men's faces and felt the tension of that moment. No longer able to witness what was sure to end in a blood bath, he turned from his peephole, fell onto his knees, and started beseeching God.

"Lord," he prayed with all the intensity of his youth, "I don't know what's happening down there. But it looks like the soldiers intend to kill the women and children. Please don't allow their lives to be taken so close to the end of the war. Put your angels around them." In anguish, he continued praying.

Down on the bridge, Helene looked around her. She knew many of the women. There was the landlady of the village inn who had been so unkind to her the first time she had been evacuated to Eschenrod. In the dead of winter, with little Susi only two months old, this woman had sent her to live in the unheated washhouse. There was the aged Frau Jost who had taken pity on her and invited her into her own home. There was Frau Straub, the mayor's wife.

There was the blond Frau Bergmann, the pastor's wife, with her five children. The youngest was only an infant and had been born on the day she received notice that her husband had been killed at the front. Helene had come to love this young woman who conducted weekly Bible studies in her home and took responsibility for the spiritual care of her husband's flock. In studying the Bible together, the two women had been able to support each other and had become very close.

Good and bad alike, there they all were. What was to become of them?

The somber-faced American commander stepped forward and announced through an interpreter. "I have asked you to assemble here because I have learned that you have committed a serious crime. Liberated Polish prisoners-of-war have revealed to us that you are hiding German soldiers in the village. As you know, this is treason. We will make you an example and execute you here on this bridge." Pale and silent the women looked at each other.

Then Frau Bergmann, her own baby in her arms, and her other children around her, stepped forward. With shaking knees she started, "Herr Commander, I vouch for the fact that there are no soldiers hiding in this village. The Poles spread this lie out of revenge. We are innocent. We are defenseless. Surely you are not going to mow us down like a field of grain?"

Gravely the commander replied, "Yes, that is just what I plan to do. You Germans did the same to your enemies."

Again Frau Bergmann spoke up, "Do you believe in God? He says, 'Revenge is mine. I will pay them back!' Do you have children at home?"

The man nodded and lowered his head.

"Does your wife know of such a plan?" she continued. "What would she think of you? Do you have faith? You know that God sees everything. Isn't it enough that my husband fell in Russia? Must you now kill us and our innocent children? I didn't think that you Americans were so hard!"

At this the commander signaled to the soldiers to lower their guns.

All this time Kurt had been praying in the attic. Long before this he had been expecting to hear gunfire. When all remained quiet, he crept up to the knothole and stared. While he could not hear what was being said, he saw immediately that the atmosphere at the bridge had changed. The soldiers had relaxed their stance. The women no longer looked paralyzed with fear.

The commander addressed them once again. "Bring me two hostages. Then I will let you go." Soon two young men volunteered. They were war casualties, home from the front, one lacking an arm, the other a leg. Seeing these young invalids convinced the commander that no German soldiers were hiding in the village. He took the young men and sent them to camps in America. They saw a good bit of the country, had wonderful food, and returned after several months telling the envious villagers of the greatest adventure in their lives.

CHAPTER 16

RETREAT

Lieutenant Gutschalk didn't bother Franz about his Bible reading any more. His animosity, however, hadn't subsided, and he bided his time to get Franz in trouble.

One Sunday afternoon the Hauptmann threw a party in honor of one of the men who'd been promoted to sergeant. Everyone was invited. Franz, who hadn't worked on Sabbath, had some bookkeeping to catch up on, so when he arrived, the party was already in full swing. There was real coffee and big platters of cake, and these rare delicacies contributed so much to the festive mood that the conversation was lively.

During a lull, Lieutenant Gutschalk suddenly turned to Franz.

"Say, Hasel," he said, "what do you think of Hitler?"

Taken by surprise, Franz blurted out the first thing that came into his head: "He is the biggest shyster under the sun!"

For a moment there was silence. Then all hell broke loose. Chairs crashed to the floor as soldiers jumped up and began pounding the wooden tables with their fists. In a flash, two old storm troopers, members of Hitler's special Sturmabteilung, the SA, had pulled their pistols and pointed them at Franz.

"This is treason of the highest degree!" they raged, in their fury spraying spittle and crumbs of cake. "We are going to shoot you! Now! Out of the way, the rest of you!"

Into the uproar thundered the Hauptmann's voice.

"Quiet here! I tell you I want quiet!" The tumult subsided, but Miekus' voice didn't.

"Soldiers," he roared, "this is a private party! We are here to celebrate. We are off duty! There will be no political discussions, and that's an order! How dare you spoil our celebration!"

Reluctantly the men sat down. The storm troopers crammed their weapons back into their holsters, cursing under their breath. Gutschalk's eyes glittered with hostility. Shortly afterward the party broke up.

Karl and Willi were the first to Franz's quarters.

"Franz," Karl said, his voice quavering slightly, "if you don't shut up, you'll get yourself killed, right here at the end of the war!"

Willi gripped Franz's shoulder in a painful squeeze. "Pull yourself together, man. Keep your own counsel!"

"I know, I know!" Franz shook himself free. "My tongue just got the better of me. I'll be more careful."

"You know that we don't like Hitler any more than you do," Willi said. "But you don't always have to say what you think."

"I *know*," Franz repeated. "Thanks for the advice."

That summer the German army began to feel as though a mammoth vise were squeezing them. Allied troops landed in France and fought their way east, while on the eastern front the Red Army pushed the Germans back step by step. The Luftwaffe had long since lost command of the air, and the Wehrmacht had never really recovered from the heavy losses of the previous winter.

In the Crimea the Pioneers themselves suffered heavy losses. The soldiers sent as replacements were often mere boys of 15 or 16. Untrained and inexperienced, they fell almost immediately. Day and night the sounds of shellfire, mortars, and cannons raged as the Russians stepped up the attacks. Fear clutched even the most seasoned soldiers. Sometimes they came to Franz shamefacedly asking for a new pair of pants—they'd filled theirs in the trenches.

When winter arrived the company finally received orders to retreat. They packed in haste and drove north, eventually reaching Odessa on the shores of the Black Sea. They were expecting a few days of rest, but word came that the Russians were close behind. Early the next morning, they fled for their lives, leaving Odessa's western suburbs while the Red Army entered the city on the east. Continuing through deep snow, the Pioneers made good time until they reached the Dnestrovskij Liman, an estuary of the Black Sea about a mile and a half wide.

Here a hodge-podge of soldiers, civilians, ox carts, trucks, wagons, and animals was lined up waiting to cross the Liman on the barge that served as a ferry. Orders came that only the military was allowed to cross, but as Franz saw the crying women and children, he said to them, "Look, if you are willing to leave all your belongings behind and just escape with your life, I'll put you on my wagons and smuggle you across. But you have to be completely quiet. It is *streng verboten* to help civilians." Gratefully, the women climbed on, a few to each wagon, and Franz hid them behind bundles and boxes. At 7:00 p.m. the last Pioneers crossed. At 9:00 p.m. the Red Army took over, capturing an entire German battalion that had been ordered to build a landing dock.

The Pioneers were ordered to find billets in the next town. But their stay wasn't an easy one—the Russians launched bombing attacks day and night. Whenever bombs fell, the Germans threw themselves to the ground, the only way they could have a chance against the horizontally spraying shrapnel.

Soon orders came to retreat further. Hastily Franz put up signs to help straggling Pioneers know where to find the rest of Unit 699. When the comrades finally caught up, many of them had lost shoes, belts, and caps in the hasty flight.

The Hauptmann assembled the company.

"Men," he addressed them after roll call, "most of you own a pair of shoes and a pair of boots. But some of you have lost everything. You have been willing to go through fire for each other. I trust that you will take care of one another's needs."

Quickly the soldiers shared their spare clothing with the ones who had nothing. Then, still hotly pursued by the Russians, the Pioneers continued west, traveling day and night until they crossed the border into Romania. The exhausted men rested for a few days in the city of Braila before heading north into the Carpathian Mountains.

During this hurried flight, Franz lost all track of time. One day he spent some moments studying the calendar, trying to orient himself. To his chagrin, he discovered that during the helter-skelter retreat, he had missed a Sabbath. During all the years of the war, it was the only Sabbath he hadn't kept.

All the way from Odessa, the Pioneers had been busy reinforcing or building bridges across the waterways so that the Wehrmacht could bring back their heavy equipment and tanks. The Germans also had thousands of horse-drawn wagons filled with munitions, clothing, food, and all the gear needed in warfare. Now orders came that only motorized vehicles were allowed on the roads, so the soldiers loaded what they could onto trucks and blew up the wagons. The horses they hitched together and led along the side of the road.

Franz still had charge of 30 horsedrawn wagons. Despite orders, he kept them on the road where traffic moved at a snail's pace. Only at the bridges were they forced off the road.

"Herr Hauptmann," Franz asked one day, "we ourselves have built this bridge, and we can't even cross it? Isn't there anything you can do about that?"

The Hauptmann sighed and shook his head. "I'm afraid not. We're going against orders as it is, keeping those horse wagons. You'll have to try to ford the river on foot."

Franz did, and guided the wagons back onto the road on the other side. High up in the Carpathians, they reached the headquarters of the General. When he saw the company with their wagons, he ran outside raging and yelling.

"Don't you know that wagons are no longer allowed on the roads? It is *streng verboten!* Where are you coming from? Who is in charge here?"

Hauptmann Miekus stepped forward. So much in the German army was *streng verboten.* "We are Pioneer Park Company 699," he said. "We are one of Hitler's 'flying battalions' and as such take orders directly from him."

"Ah, so," the General said, "that's different, of course. I'll tell you what. You pull your wagons off the road here and wait till nighttime. You may proceed from 6:00 p.m. to 6:00 a.m. but not during the day. Otherwise I will have a riot on my hands."

Content with this arrangement, the Pioneers made camp while thousands of soldiers rushed by. No one understood how they could be so relaxed with the Russians on their heels. The company ate at 5:00 p.m., then packed their belongings, and promptly at 6:00 took off like lightning. Since the roads were empty at night, their travel actually proceeded faster than the motorized vehicles that moved by day.

High in the mountains they reached a signpost: "Budapest, Hungary— 897 miles (1,495 kilometers)." They figured they could cover 30 miles (50 kilometers) per night and reach Budapest in 20 days.

As their nightly journey continued, they became aware of an eerie glow on the horizon in the direction of Budapest.

Willi sidled up to Franz and asked, "Franz, what do you suppose that is?"

"I think the whole city is burning," Franz responded.

The Pioneers rushed on, and reached Budapest in a record time of 18 days. There they had a big surprise: the whole city was brightly illuminated at night. No blackout here. No air raid warden walked the streets at night looking for chinks of light that might endanger a whole neighborhood. It was a sight the soldiers had not seen in years. In fact, the city was little affected by the war, and the Hungarians treated the Germans kindly.

Hauptmann Miekus decided to proceed with trucks only. Many other units had had to abandon their vehicles already because of lack of fuel, but thanks to the gasoline the Pioneers had hoarded for 18 months, they had plenty of fuel to get all the way home. They loaded their belongings onto trucks and gave their wagons and horses to grateful companies who had no transportation.

The Pioneers were ordered to build a bridge across the Danube for the sea of German troops flooding back. The bridge was completed in four days. The retreat became more and more hectic. At the point of exhaustion, the Pioneers reached Hungary's Balaton Lake.

But there was to be no rest for the weary men. At 2:00 the following morning they were awakened by gunshots.

Rattled, a bleary-eyed Hauptmann crashed into Franz's room. "Hasel. What's that noise?"

Seconds before, Franz had returned from a scouting expedition. "It's the Russians shooting with trench mortars, sir. They're only a few hundred yards away!"

"Wh–what should I do?"

"Sir." Franz kept his voice level and as confident as possible. "Do you want to become a Russian prisoner-of-war? Order immediate departure, or we are lost!"

"I can't do that. I have no orders from above!"

"Herr Hauptmann, we cannot wait for orders! This is a time for independent action!"

In the pitch-black night the Pioneers took off. Three hours later they met the commander of the battalion out on horseback looking for them.

"Am I glad to see you!" he yelled. "We couldn't get word to you. We didn't know where you were. You are the last company of the battalion to catch up."

On they rushed, eventually crossing the border into Austria. Because the Russians had already occupied the area around Vienna, the battalion was forced to take a detour that took them to Graz on the southern border of Austria. Soon they were ordered to swing straight north to Bruck an der Mur and from there north again to St. Poelten. After only a week orders came to go south again to Mariazell. There was no more logic to their movements. The roads were clogged with Wehrmacht surging north or south. It was impossible to cover any distance.

Franz, who had lived and colporteured in Austria for nine years, went to the Hauptmann.

"Sir, I know this country like the palm of my hand. I can get us to Mariazell on back roads if you like."

Relief washed over the weary commander's face. "Absolutely, Hasel. Take over the leadership!"

The Pioneers left the main thoroughfares and crawled along unpaved roads up and down the Alps. Yet they reached Mariazell before anyone else, and were able to billet themselves in a large hotel. While the company took stations and held back the Russians, Franz assembled his office and set up the only radio the company had left. For months he had been listening to the enemy station—the only way to get reliable news about the war's progress.

On Sunday Franz strolled through Mariazell, a famous pilgrimage town. At the pilgrimage church the sermon had just started. Curiously Franz listened in.

"Good people," the priest was just saying, "don't worry. If we can't get into heaven through the main gate, God always has a back door through which we can sneak in. We'll all get there somehow."

Franz had heard enough. Shaking his head, he moved on.

On May 1, 1945, while Franz was listening to the radio news, he saw Lieutenant Gutschalk walk by outside. Franz yanked open the window and put his head out.

"Peter," he called. "Peter, have you heard the news? I want to express my condolences."

The lieutenant whirled, his face chalk white. "What is it?" he quavered. "What happened? Have you received bad news of my family?"

"No, Peter, it's worse than that. Your god has just died. He killed himself yesterday."

Peter's face turned from white to a beet red. He shot Franz a hate-filled look and walked on.

A few days later when several men were clustered around the radio, Miekus entered. An announcement was just blasting out of the speaker: "Achtung, Achtung! We are demanding full surrender of the German Wehrmacht! Give yourselves up! Surrender your weapons!"

Miekus was enraged.

"Who turned the enemy station on? It is *streng verboten!*" he roared.

"Herr Hauptmann," Franz said respectfully, "there is no other station left. We are surrounded by enemies. The only two pockets left that are still held by Germans are Prague and here in Mariazell."

"I tell you, Hasel," snapped Miekus, "we are not going to lose the war. This is all enemy propaganda."

"What will we win the war with, sir?" Franz asked, wondering whether Miekus actually believed what he was saying. "We have no more food, clothing, or ammunition. For months now we have eaten bread that consists of 50 percent sawdust. And we can't get more supplies because the enemy is in control of everything."

Miekus had been open when alone with Franz, but now he betrayed a rare moment of indecision before others of the rank and file.

"You have a point there," he said in a low voice. "Frankly, I'm so confused, I don't know what to do."

"Why not go to the commander of the Battalion and get directions?"

Half an hour later, Miekus telephoned Franz.

"Hasel, call our soldiers back from the front and burn all secret documents. Save the non-classified files."

Franz immediately sent messengers to recall his comrades from their stations and had them load the vehicles. In the courtyard he built a roaring fire and tossed in all the files, the non-classified along with the secret ones.

Miekus strode in. "What are you doing? You were only to burn the secret documents."

"Sir," Franz said, "The war is over. We'll have no more use for these things, and we don't want the Russians to find them. Let's destroy them and keep only our money and our service records."

Lieutenant Gutschalk stepped to the fire to rescue the files. "We are never going to capitulate!"

"Lieutenant," Franz said, "you need to learn something important. The tide has turned. Up to now you called the shots, but you can't harm me anymore. Because of my Christian beliefs, you have wanted to do away with me all during the war. Now those same Christian beliefs are going to be your salvation because I'm not going to turn you in for war crimes."

Just then, a voice boomed over the radio, "Germany has surrendered! I repeat, Germany has surrendered!"

It was May 8, 1945.

The Hauptmann called headquarters, then assembled his men and told them, "Men, the surrender is official. The enemies have signed a treaty that states that all German soldiers who cross the river Enns by 11:00 a.m. tomorrow morning will become American prisoners-of-war. The ones who don't make it will fall into Russian hands. From now on it's every man for himself. Take the vehicles and fly. Good luck to you!"

Franz, Karl, Willi, and Sergeant Erich decided to stick together. They pulled out at 10:00 a.m. The Russians entered Mariazell 30 minutes later. Hordes of Germans were already crawling over the high Alpine passes all heading toward the common goal—to reach the Americans before it was too late. If a wagon lost a wheel, it was heaved over the cliffs. When trucks ran out of gas, 20 men immediately surrounded it and sent it to the same destination. Sometimes an hour was lost before the road was cleared again.

During these involuntary stops, Franz and Karl climbed down the mountainside and scavenged among the discarded vehicles. They returned with a cache of canned goods, cigarettes, and armfuls of cowhides. They loaded the things onto their own truck and continued on.

One or the other would glance at his watch and anxiously calculate the distance yet to be covered. The next delay came when the road ran alongside a clear mountain stream full of trout. Looking down, Willi said, "Hey guys, let's shoot some fish!" By the time the column started up again, Karl and Willi had a nice catch of fresh trout.

Finally, from the top of a mountain, they saw the river glistening in the distance like a silver ribbon. Would they make it?

The defeated Wehrmacht all but stampeded to the distant goal. At 10:30 a.m. Franz, Karl, Willi, and Erich crossed the bridge over the river Enns. For them the war was over.

American soldiers met them on the other side. "Stop!" they said in simple German, and gestured to one pile. "Weapons here," they said, gesturing to one pile. "Ammunition there."

Franz unbuttoned his holster and tossed his wooden "revolver" on the heap.

Willi's eyes started from their sockets. "Franz," he asked, "What on earth is that thing?"

"That's my gun," said Franz, eyes twinkling. "I had it made in Poland and got rid of my real one there."

"Are you crazy?"

"You see, I didn't ever want to be in a position where I would be tempted to shoot someone."

Sergeant Erich stared even harder at Franz. This was the man he'd chosen to be his guardian angel during the entire war!

The Americans waved them on. Pointing west, they said, "Braunau. Prison camp."

The men understood, but now there was no more hurry. They could relax at last, because finally they were safe. They drove a few kilometers, then stopped for lunch where over an open campfire Willi and Karl roasted the fresh trout. What a treat it was!

The following day at noon, just before their gasoline ran out, they reached the camp and joined the 140,000 German prisoners-of-war already there. At the time the retreat had started, the Pioneers had been among the troops farthest from Germany; they had covered the greatest distance. Now they had reached their last goal of the war: to be in the hands of the Americans and not the Russians.

CHAPTER 17

RETURN HOME

When Karl, Willi, Erich, and Franz drove through the gates of the prison camp, they cheered their good fortune to have fallen into the hands of the humane Americans.

"I'll stay with the truck," Franz said to the other three. "Why don't you guys go look for other Pioneers?"

"Lord," he prayed, while the busy camp life bustled past his windshield, "You have kept Your promises! You alone deserve praise and thanks for bringing me alive through the dangers of war. I will never forget Your goodness." Then he rummaged in the back of the truck, got out the box that contained the army records, and started balancing the accounts and closing the books.

"Achtung! Achtung!" blared the loudspeaker the next morning, calling the battalion of which the Pioneers were a part to line up for roll call. Several units showed up, but the entire fourth unit was missing-in-action and presumed dead.

Not all the Pioneers had reached camp either. Hauptmann Miekus told the remaining ones to show up at Franz's barracks that evening after supper. Here Franz gave each man the last service pay due him and the Wehrpass containing his service record.

"Look, Willi," he said. "All the men are hungry. The Americans just don't have the kitchen staff to prepare food for so many soldiers. Why don't you do the cooking for our own company again?"

"Good idea," Willi said, and the next day he went to the camp kitchen and brought back vegetables and potatoes. These he mixed into a thick stew, and supplemented it with pancakes made from flour they'd brought all the way from Romania.

Meanwhile Franz went to the cashier of the battalion and turned over the accounting records and the remaining cash for which he received a receipt. He had done his duty faithfully and well. Then he and Karl divided the other goods among the men: sugar, sunflower oil, and enough cigarettes to give each man a suitcase full.

"Attention, please!" the loudspeaker crackled a little over a week later. "Would all men going to Frankfurt report for discharge! All men going to Frankfurt, please report immediately!"

"Karl," Franz said, "I'm not going yet. I'm going to see that heap of rubble soon enough, and I want to finish up here. I am not packed yet anyway. Tonight I'll get my things together so I'm ready for the next call." Karl, Willi, and Erich also decided to stay.

After supper Franz carefully laid out his belongings. In addition to the food items, he had brand-new pairs of pants and boots he had bought in Romania—"my discharge clothes," he had told the others. Then he packed his rucksack, his bread bag, and laundry sack with his belongings. Out of burlap he sewed a cover for a five-gallon canister filled with sunflower oil so that only the handle showed. When he finished, his goods weighed 150 pounds.

Two days later the loudspeaker again called for men returning to Frankfurt. The four friends ran to say goodbye to Hauptmann Miekus who, as a higher officer, was required to stay. Then they picked up their things and started on the five-mile hike to the discharge center.

After only a short distance, Franz stopped. He was panting, and sweat was pouring down his face.

"Friends, we'll never make it like this. Karl, run back and borrow our company's bicycle. We can return it later."

Karl soon returned. They hung the rucksacks on the handlebars, draped the laundry sacks over the frame, and tied the oil containers to the narrow carrier on the back. Franz steered, and Karl pushed while the other two kept things balanced. Now they made good progress. Other soldiers found their loads too heavy and left most of their things behind.

Finally they reached the discharge camp. Here a German major with a megaphone ordered everybody to form a column. When he saw the four with their bicycle, he yelled, "What are you doing with a bike? Aren't you going to line up?" Quickly they laid the bike on the ground and fell in. Then he barked, "All SS men, step to the left." Several men stepped out and were sent back to the main camp with a guard. The rest were led to a train in which the discharge center had been set up.

In the first car a doctor conducted a physical exam. After the men undressed, he took their blood pressure and listened to their heart and lungs. Finally, he said to each one, "Lift your right arm. Good. Lift your left arm. Good. You may get dressed."

Franz, totally confused by this maneuver, watched curiously as the others went through the routine. When it was Sergeant Erich's turn to lift his arms, Franz noticed that he had a number tattooed on the underside of his arm.

"Aha," the doctor said, "we caught one! SS men will not be released. Please wait outside for a guard."

"Erich," Franz said when the four men had gathered back at the bicycle. "Erich, I never knew you belonged to the SS. You are not even a supporter of the Nazis. What happened?"

Erich sighed. "I joined the SS years before the war," he said. "But then I got disillusioned and quit. When the war came, I volunteered to fight in the regular army. I guess I'm going back to camp, so I'll return the bike." Sadly the friends said goodbye.

Franz, Karl, and Willi took their discharge papers to the next railroad car for final approval.

"Stand at attention," said the American colonel behind the table.

The men stiffened. Out of habit, Karl, who had been a strong opponent of the Führer, stretched out his right arm and said, "Heil Hitler!"

The colonel glared at him, shocked and revolted. "Discharge denied!" he growled.

"Now," he said, turning to Franz. "Give me your papers." After glancing at them, he said in fluent German, "I see in your service record a notation that you are to be court martialled after the war."

"Yes, sir." Franz had studied this entry closely.

"What did you do to earn this?"

"I refused an order for religious reasons. I am a Seventh-day Adventist, and I keep the Sabbath holy as the Bible asks us to do. Once, on my day of rest, there was an attack, and I refused to do duty because it was the Sabbath."

"Wait a minute." The colonel's eyebrows and voice showed his incredulity. "You can't be serious. All through the war you kept the Sabbath in the Nazi army, and you survived?"

"Yes, sir. God protected me, even in the German army."

"That's amazing," said the colonel. "I'm a Jew myself, by the way. But even in the American army I don't keep the Sabbath because it's too difficult."

"Colonel," Franz said boldly, "I recommend that you keep the Sabbath."

"I suppose I really should," the man responded. Still shaking his head in amazement, he continued with the interview. "What is your occupation?"

"I am a minister of the gospel and a colporteur. I sell religious books door-to-door."

"Sorry. We're only allowed to release farm workers at this time. Do you know anything about farming?"

"Well, from age 6 to 14 I lived with my grandfather. He was a farmer in southern Germany. I know how to do all the farm tasks."

The colonel shook his head. "I can't make that work. Your experience isn't current." Suddenly he had an idea. "Say, do you by any chance have a garden?"

"Yes, we have a small garden in Frankfurt."

"That'll do it!" He scrawled something on one of the papers. "I hereby discharge you to work in the vineyard of the Lord!" Beaming, he handed the papers back to Franz.

On them he had written "Agricultural Inspector."

Soon American trucks arrived. Franz was the first one on, and as Willi handed up their luggage, Franz quickly stowed it under a seat so it wouldn't be so conspicuous. They were on the way: Braunau, Regensburg, Nuernberg, Frankfurt. The men learned that every few days a convoy of trucks drove to Luxembourg to transport food supplies to the prison camp. On the return trip, the trucks were loaded with released prisoners-of-war. Two drivers, taking turns, reached Frankfurt in 24 hours. On the city's outskirts the men got off.

It was May 21, 1945. Franz was free.

Of the original company of 1,200 Pioneers, only seven survived; only three of those were not wounded. Franz Hasel, the man with the wooden pistol, was one of the three.

Barely two weeks earlier, the wild ringing of Eschenrod church bells awakened Helene. Outside she could hear people running and shouting. Herr Straub pounded on her door yelling, "Frau Hasel, Frau Hasel. Come down!"

Helene threw on some clothes and rushed out. In the street she saw Germans and Americans laughing and crying and embracing each other. It was May 8, 1945. The war was over. The villagers were told that Hitler had committed suicide, that Germany had capitulated, and that the Allied Forces had divided the country into four parts. Eschenrod was in the American occupied zone, and until a government could be established, they were to obey American regulations. And until further notice, none of the evacuees from the cities were to return home.

"Children, children, come into the house," Helene called to them. Back in their room, the little family knelt with grateful hearts and thanked God for bringing them safely through the war.

"But where's Papa?" whispered Lotte as the prayer concluded. "Is he still alive?"

"Please, God," Helene prayed. "Bring him back to us."

Slowly the days and weeks passed. Things weren't that much different from the war's final weeks, except that no longer did the burning city of Frankfurt cast an orange glow against the night sky.

The children attended school and helped in the fields since there were so few people left who could work. No word had come from Papa in a long, long time. His last letter had been posted in Russia's Caucasus Mountains, and it was being whispered that German soldiers caught there had been sent to Siberian labor camps.

On the outskirts of Frankfurt, Franz and Willi stared at the heap of luggage piled on the sidewalk around them.

"Willi, there is no way we can carry this," the older man said. "You stay here and guard it while I try to find something to haul it in."

Franz was shocked to see the destruction of the city. Later he learned that 80 percent of Frankfurt had been leveled. Here and there women were digging through the rubble for still-useable utensils. A boy was knocking mortar off bricks so that they could be recycled.

Coming toward him, Franz spotted an old man pulling a wooden handcart. This was exactly what he needed.

"Excuse me, is this your cart?"

"Yes."

"We have just been released from prison camp. We have a lot of things to transport. If you'll lend us your cart, I'll give you your choice of 100 Marks, or five pounds of cigarette tobacco, or half a liter of sunflower oil. We'll return the cart in a few days."

The man studied him closely. "Well, I'm on my way home from the train station. I found some coal there—if you know what I mean."

"No problem," Franz responded. "I'll accompany you home and help you unload the coal."

"Jawohl," the man agreed. "By the way, I would like to have the oil."

The man never asked Franz's name or address, but willingly loaned him the wagon. When Franz took it back to Willi, they loaded their belongings and covered them with a tarp to protect them from prying eyes. Then, pulling and pushing, they made their way through the rubble.

"Oh-oh," Willi said. "I see that we're not going to make good time."

"Why's that?"

"Look who's coming—the wives."

Seeing the soldiers, women converged from all directions. Their emaciated bodies and tattered clothes told the story of the ravages of war at home. Silently they looked at the men with eyes full of hope and dread.

Then the questions began.

"Where do you come from?"

"We are from the eastern front," Willi said.

"My husband was there too," one of the women said, and others echoed with their own questions, calling out name after name. "Have you seen Georg Schneider? Do you have any news of Heinrich Gerber?"

"Look, ladies, be reasonable," the two men responded, "we can't know everybody who fought in Russia."

Franz turned to Willi. "If this doesn't stop, we'll never get home. From now on we say we recently arrived from Austria."

Another woman headed in their direction.

"Where are you from?"

"We just got here from Austria."

"My youngest boy, Hans Kimmel, was there. I haven't heard from him in months. My other three sons fell in Russia. Do you know anything?"

"No, we are sorry. We don't know that name. We have no news."

"Franz, this isn't going to work," Willi said. "Let's try saying we just arrived from prison camp."

American soldiers were stationed at all the bridges they had to cross. Each time they had to show their papers. The documents were in order, but the GI's eyed the cart suspiciously. However, no one objected.

Another woman came running after them.

"Where are you from?"

"We are just released from prisoner-of-war camp."

"What unit were you with?"

"Pioneer Park Company 699."

"My husband was too. Do you know Ludwig Keller?"

"Frau Keller," said Franz, "your husband was on the same truck with us. He may already be standing at your front door and can't get in!"

With a scream of joy the woman turned and ran.

"Willi," Franz said a little later, "we'd better go to my apartment first. It's still all the way across town, but it's closer than yours."

"Great, if that's all right with you."

In the evening, they finally reached their goal. After seeing section after section of the city leveled, it almost came as a shock to see the block of six large apartment buildings intact. Like a huge fortress they rose above the rubble.

As Franz and Willi hauled the cart into the entry, a neighbor stuck her head out the door.

"Herr Hasel, you are back! Welcome, a thousand times welcome! You're one of the first men to return."

"Frau Jaeckel, I am so happy to see you."

"Your family is not here. They are in Eschenrod."

Franz was befuddled for a moment. "Eschenrod?"

"You know. The village in the Vogelsberg Mountains."

He nodded and sighed. "Thank you very much. And a good day to you."

Franz opened the door with his key he'd kept all through the war. He and Willi unloaded the cart, and while Willi took a bath, Franz looked the apartment over. The windows were broken, and the curtains flew in the wind, but nothing was missing. The furniture, bedding, dishes, books, even Franz's pre-war motorcycle parked in the spare room—they were all there. Later Franz learned that Polish prisoners-of-war had stayed in the elementary school a quarter mile away, and when they'd been liberated they had looted freely and taken anything that was not nailed down. God had evidently held His hand over the Hasel apartment.

Finally Franz bathed and shaved, and after they'd eaten a meal, the men retired for the night. Oh the luxury to be in one's own bed again!

Next morning, the friends said a warm goodbye, and Willi left for his home in the Taunus Mountains, leaving half his things in the apartment to be picked up later.

Knowing his family was probably quite safe in the remote village, Franz walked the eight miles downtown to the conference office to report back. The conference president welcomed him.

"Brother Hasel, you're the first conference employee back from the war!" he exclaimed. "Could you help us a while as a pastor? We are in desperate need, because many of my men have lost their lives. There's no publishing work at the moment. In fact, we don't even know if the publishing house is still standing because there are no trains, no mail, no phones."

"I tell you what," said Franz. "If God needs me to be a pastor, I'll be a pastor. But my family isn't here. I haven't seen them in a long, long time. Let me go and bring them back, and I'll be ready to start the first of July."

"Oh, Brother Hasel, you can't imagine how grateful I am. God bless you!"

The following day Franz returned the handcart to its owner, along with the promised oil, and began the 40-mile journey to Eschenrod. The miles stretched endlessly. He spent the night in a barn, then continued on.

Finally a signpost said "Eschenrod 5 km." Franz stopped at a clear brook in the woods, cleaned up, and shaved. When he heard a wagon rattling by on the road, he hailed the driver.

"Say, are you going to Eschenrod?"

The driver nodded. "I live there."

"I'm just back from the war," said Franz. "My wife is one of the evacuees there. Do you know a Frau Hasel?"

"Oh yes, she is staying with the mayor. Here," the driver said, climbing down. "Put your bags on the wagon. There's not quite room enough for both of us, so I'll walk with you the rest of the way."

Still some distance from the village, Franz saw a boy coming along the dusty road. The child shaded his eyes against the sun and looked toward them. Suddenly, he started running.

"Papa!" he screamed. "Papa! You're back!" He flung himself into his father's arms.

"Gerd?" Franz said in a trembly voice. "Is this my little Gerd?"

"Oh, I am so glad!" Gerd gasped. "I have been walking along this road every day hoping to be the first one to see you! Oh, Papa!"

The driver chuckled. "Hop up on the wagon, son," he said. "And I guess I'd better get up beside you and make sure you don't run away with the horses."

"I'll walk," said Franz. "I couldn't sit still a moment."

On that cool May afternoon Helene sat on the rough-hewn bench outside the farmhouse, shelling peas. The older children were out playing while little Susi was floating pea shells in a pan of water.

In the distance she saw the neighbor returning from market in his wagon pulled by two horses. A tall, deeply tanned man followed some distance behind. Helene didn't know him, and wondered where he was headed. Just then she noticed Gerd riding on the wagon seat beside the neighbor and smiling proudly.

When they came alongside, the wagon pulled up, and the neighbor called, "Frau Hasel, I am bringing you a visitor. I hope you are happy about it."

Mildly surprised, Helene answered, "It was very kind of you to give Gerd a ride."

By this time the tall stranger had caught up and was lifting some baggage down from the wagon. He approached while Helene stared into his dark brown face. Then the stranger started laughing, and Helene recognized him.

"Children!" she shouted joyfully when she could catch her breath.

"Children! Come quickly—something wonderful has happened. Our Papa has come back! Our Papa is home!"

After six years of war and separation, the Hasel family was together again.

CHAPTER 18

WINTER RESCUE

Helene," said Franz one day, "I think it's best that you and the children go home to Frankfurt while I stay here for awhile and help the farmers harvest their hay."

"I'm not looking forward to the trip," she said, "but maybe that's best."

For the last time they packed their belongings and loaded up their bikes and the baby buggy. Again they had to make the 40-mile journey on foot—there weren't many trains running yet—but finally they arrived at their apartment. Frankfurt was devastated, but things seemed far more hopeful than they ever had before.

"Bring our beds up from the basement, boys," said Helene.

"Whew! No more air raids, no more bombings," said Kurt.

"No more air raid shelters," muttered Gerd, shuddering as he thought of the dark, tightly-packed nights he'd spent in them.

Franz arrived two weeks later. He brought oil, butter, potatoes, and bread that the grateful farmers had given him.

The next day Franz went downtown to the Conference office. There he learned that the German publishing house, the Advent Verlag in Hamburg, had been destroyed and that all colporteur work had come to a standstill. The conference immediately hired Franz to be the pastor of several churches on the outskirts of Frankfurt because at that point no one knew which conference workers had survived and which had perished. No Adventist pastors had returned yet from the army.

Using the bike returned to Helene by the American soldier, Jim, in Eschenrod, Franz traveled distances up to 75 miles until he had visited all the church members in his district. Often he spent the night with them, and sometimes he was gone for several days or even a week.

No family he talked to had been unaffected by the war. Homes had been destroyed by bombs, belongings had been looted. Husband, sons, brothers, uncles, cousins had been killed in action. And many of the families did not know yet the fate of their men. Some, like the Hasels' Onkel Fritz, were missing in action, and most had not yet returned from the war.

And everyone was poor—farming and manufacturing were at a standstill. Silent, bitter, defeated men stood in endless unemployment lines hoping for work.

Church members living in the country had no money to pay their tithe, but sometimes they were able to give Franz some food. Since the conference could pay Franz only very small wages, they told him that he could use the food as a supplement to his salary. One time he came home with 100 pounds of chicken feed. Helene cooked a portion for breakfast each day, and the family ate the scratchy stuff like porridge. It left their voices hoarse most of the day.

The first winter arrived. There was never enough of anything; food, clothing, and coal were still rationed. The worsening weather meant that Franz no longer could ride the bike, so he had to go by train, and because of poor connections and overcrowdedness, he was gone even more often than before.

"Boys! Boys!"

One icy day in November Franz rushed in the door with news. "Get the wooden handcart and the bicycles out of the basement, and find all the empty sacks you can!" While he ate some hot soup, he told the family that the road in Oberursel, 10 miles away, was being torn up and that people were allowed to cart away the broken pieces of blacktop and use them for heating.

For the next three days Franz, Kurt, and Gerd traveled back and forth from Oberursel. Each night they returned frozen and dirty, but with the cart and bikes loaded with asphalt. When Helene threw the first chunks of blacktop in the furnace, Lotte started crying.

"It smells like a tar pit," she sobbed, "and it's giving me a headache."

"As long as we stay warm this winter, we'll get used to the smell," Helene comforted. No sooner was Lotte quieted down than Gerd came running in.

"The stove's leaking," he said. "Come and see."

When Helene opened the door, she saw that the asphalt had melted and completely clogged the inside of the furnace. A trickle of liquid tar oozed out its front door. They doused the fire and, when the stove had cooled down, spent hours scraping the inside until it could be used again. The blacktop had to be thrown away.

After supper one February evening Helene looked over at Franz.

"This is it," she said. "Our weekly food ration cards are used up. We have only half a loaf of bread left, and it's going to be five days before we can get more. What are we going to do?"

Franz thought for a moment. "I have to conduct a funeral tomorrow," he finally said. "Do you suppose you could go to Eschenrod and 'hamster' some food?" "Hamstering" was the term Germans had coined when they talked about going to the country to beg or buy food from farmers. Just like a hamster stuffs its cheeks and carries food to its nest, the people were stuffing bags and pockets to bring food to their children.

Helene reluctantly agreed, and Franz left early the next morning for the funeral. As Kurt came into the kitchen, Helene was getting ready to go also. He looked from her to the large rucksack and the two shopping bags in a heap on the floor.

"Mutti," he said, "I am coming with you. You know you will have a hard time getting through all that snow."

"No, that would make us too conspicuous. Remember, hamstering is technically illegal. But it's not stealing, and we've got to live somehow."

"Could I follow you at a distance or something?"

Helene shook her head. "No, Kurt. You're the oldest, and you need to supervise the children."

While Helene pulled on her boots, she gave Kurt some final instructions: "All of you must stay home from school today and tomorrow. There is a little bit of bread left. Ration it carefully, and eat it slowly. Wrap yourselves in blankets so you stay warm. Papa may not be able to get back for several days, but I promise I will be home tomorrow night with food for you."

She strapped on the rucksack and picked up the two handbags. "You go back to bed and sleep a little longer. Don't worry if I am late. The trains are not punctual."

"Mutti," said Kurt, "we'll be praying for you." They embraced quickly, and she was gone.

Even at this early hour, the railway station in Frankfurt was teeming. Like Helene, many people were on their way to the country foraging for food, and the train to Eschenrod was packed by the time she arrived. She pushed her way inside a car, grateful even for standing room, and glad she didn't have to stand on the drafty platform between cars, or even on the steps outside hanging onto the handrails, as some did.

Wedged tightly into the compartment, Helene relaxed. She looked at her silent fellow travelers, all swaying in unison with the chugging of the steam engine, their closeness providing warmth. They were mostly middle aged, a few young, a few very old, no children. The men had stubbly beards and frayed collars, and many wore a black armband that said *Kriegsversehrt*—war invalid. The women wore coats that were ill fitting and unbecoming—free handouts that had gratefully been accepted by a defeated people.

It had been snowing in Frankfurt, but as the train approached the Vogelsberg Mountains, the clouds broke apart. When it pulled into the station, Helene breathed deeply the brisk fresh morning air as she set out on her two-mile walk to the village. Though it was very cold, the air was clear. Occasionally the sun came through and made the spruce trees with their thick covering of snow sparkle like jewels. In the forest nothing stirred. No birds sang, no bees hummed, no frogs rustled in the dry leaves—nothing but cold, crystal winter loveliness. At one point Helene had to stop and thank God for giving such beauty. Then some crows cawed harshly, and jerked her out of her reverie.

When she stepped out of the woods, the snow started softly falling again. She hoped that the Josts would keep her for the night. As she approached the house, Frau Jost stepped out of the stable, a steaming bucket of milk in each hand.

"Frau Hasel, is that you? I can't believe it! You must be frozen. Come in and rest."

Herr Jost was sitting at the kitchen table reading the newspaper. Hearing unfamiliar footsteps, he turned, then jumped up and grabbed Helene's hand.

"Welcome back!" he cried. "How are the children? How is the little one?"

Helene sat down on one of the wooden chairs and began to tell about the children.

Suddenly Herr Jost glanced at Helene's bags. "You have come for food. Are things really bad in the city?" As Frau Jost set some thick slabs of bread, a ball of butter, and some hot milk on the table, Helene recounted the hardships of those first postwar months in the city.

"Well," Frau Jost said, "don't you worry about a thing. We will see to it that you can take home a good supply of food." She started bustling around and presently set out oil, butter, flour, bread, sugar, eggs, potatoes, and many other things. Then she sent Helene to the Jost relatives. When they learned of the hunger in the city, they also loaded her till she looked like St. Nikolaus at Christmas packed with gifts for the children. Hunger would be banished for many weeks.

She returned to the Jost farm where she had been invited to spend the night. Frau Jost insisted that she retire early and promised to wake her in time to catch the horse-drawn sled that made the trip to the railroad station early each morning.

The small chamber beside the kitchen with its thick feather bed was inviting. The heat from the large green tile stove in the kitchen seeped through the wall and took the edge off the bitter cold. With a full heart, Helene knelt beside the bed thanking her heavenly Father for fulfilling her needs and asking for protection for the children and herself the next day. Then she climbed into bed and quickly fell into a deep sleep.

When she heard Frau Jost's knock on the door, it seemed impossible that the night had already passed. Frau Jost stuck her head in the door. "Frau Hasel, you might as well stay in bed."

"Why?" Helene murmured, still half asleep.

"It will be impossible for you to leave today. It's been snowing all night. The sled won't go to the station this morning. Even the snowplow won't go out until the storm stops."

Helene stepped to the window, and her heart sank. Deep white drifts covered everything in sight, and enormous flakes still fell from the sky.

Desperately she turned to the old woman. "I've got to leave," she said. "The children have no food, and I promised them I would be back tonight. They'll be so worried if I don't come. God will watch over me, and if I leave right away, I can get there in time for the afternoon train to Frankfurt."

"Frau Hasel, you have at least 80 pounds of food, and there's no way you can walk. If something happened to you, I would never forgive myself."

"I must go," said Helene firmly.

Seeing that Helene could not be talked out of her plan, Frau Jost fixed a sturdy breakfast of boiled potatoes with buttermilk, bread, homemade plum butter, and Ersatzkaffee. While the younger woman ate, Frau Jost went into her pantry and returned with dried apples, pears, prunes, nuts, and a whole poppy seed cake. "A little treat for the children," she said as she stuffed every nook in the bulging bags.

Helene was unable to restrain her tears of gratitude. "How will I ever be able to thank you?"

"No need to thank me," said Frau Jost, her own eyes wet with tears. "I am glad to help. Just pass the favor on to someone else when you are able to. May God protect you."

Helene embraced the old couple, and then set out. When she reached the bend in the road, she turned back one last time. They still stood watching in their doorway. Helene paused for a moment taking in the scene: the cozy village under its covering of snow, the quaint cottage where she had spent so many anguished months during the war. She lifted her hand, and the couple responded with a last wave. Then she turned and started up the hill. Though she did not know it then, it was to be the last time she saw the Josts.

All the while it snowed and snowed, and soon Helene couldn't see 10 steps in front of her. Her feet seemed heavier and heavier, and her load pressed down. "Dear God," she prayed again, "help me, give me strength."

Her limbs ached as she painfully pulled each foot out of the deep snow. Her breathing became labored, and the icy air cut into her lungs like knives. She reached the hill leading into the woods, and as she ascended her burden weighed her down even more.

Lord help me. Oh, who will help me?

Suddenly she could go no further. Her knees started to buckle under her, and in panic she staggered to a high milestone by the side of the road. *One mile to the station,* she read.

Wearily she leaned against the stone, resting the rucksack on top of it. As her bags slipped from her hands, they almost disappeared in the deep snow. She shut her eyes for a moment.

I must not fall asleep. I must not fall asleep. All I need is a few minutes to catch my breath, and then I'll continue..

Her thoughts wandered to her hungry children at home. Again she closed her eyes, then jerked them open. *If I fall asleep, I might never wake again.* She was beginning to feel heavy and oh-so-comfortably warm. Once more, her eyes closed, and this time they stayed that way.

The snow settled on her. Soon, still leaning against the signpost, she looked like a gnarled tree stump, a part of the noiseless landscape. She started to dream, at first seeing herself standing in the snow with fluffy snowflakes swirling out of a leaden sky. The next instant, she was enveloped by a circle of light, and when she looked again, it was no longer snowflakes but white clad angels that encircled her.

Such peace, she thought, such wonderful peace. . . .

The rumble of an approaching motor roused her, and she jerked awake. A diesel truck was laboring up the hill. She tried to raise her hand to flag him down, but her stiff limbs would not obey her. In despair she saw the truck continue on its slow course, and sleep washed over her once more.

A voice suddenly said, *"Now you will see a miracle of God."*

"Will I get home again?" she asked the voice.

And the answer came, *"Your suffering is almost over—only another moment."*

A heavy hand shook her by the shoulder. Each time she tried to raise her head, it drooped forward again. The shaking, the jolting, went on and on.

Leave me alone, she thought. *I'm so wonderfully warm, and I have no energy to move.*

"Wake up, wake up," a rough voice kept saying. "You must wake up. You are about to freeze."

Annoyed, she finally opened her eyes to see a man standing in front of her.

"I parked my truck at the top of the hill," he said. "I couldn't stop right here or I never would have made it up. You come with me now, and I'll give you a ride."

Mechanically she tried to stand up straight, but her stiff body did not cooperate. Realizing she needed help, the driver took her bags and rucksack and started up the hill. Then he returned and half dragged, half carried her to the cab. He gave her a drink from his thermos of hot tea, wrapped blankets around her, and turned the heat up high before he continued his journey.

"That was a close call," the man said, "I do believe you almost froze to death. I nearly missed you, you were so covered with snow. What are you doing out anyway on a day like this?"

Helene was beginning to thaw out. She told him about her four hungry children at home and her effort to get food.

"Thank you so much for picking me up. God sent you to help me," she concluded. "I know I shouldn't have rested. But I was so tired. As soon as I stopped, warmth flooded through me. I just could not stay awake. It would be a great help if you could take me to the train station."

"You know," he said, "the interesting thing is that I never come this way. Today is the first time I've been along this route. As far as taking you to the train station, that's going to be useless. I know from reliable sources that all trains are being searched. Any black market food is confiscated. It would be a shame to lose it after all you've been through to get it. Where do you live, anyway?"

"In Eschersheim. It's a suburb of Frankfurt."

"I tell you what. I'll just take you there. Eschersheim is not much out of my way."

Gratefully Helene accepted. She now looked at the driver more carefully. Middle-aged, nondescript, coarse clothing, rough hands, brown hair streaked with gray, probably married with children himself. He now became rather taciturn and began responding to her small talk with monosyllables. Finally, she gave up and dozed off. She woke when the truck stopped.

"Well, here we are," said the driver, turning off the motor. He lifted out her bags, then helped her down the steep step.

She took his hand gratefully. "I just don't know how to thank you enough."

"I'm glad I found you before it was too late. In the future you must stay home in such bad weather. Now I must be on my way."

With a final nod of his head he climbed back into the cab. She stooped to slip the rucksack straps over her shoulders, groggily wondering how she had gotten there. Then she turned to have a last glance at the disappearing truck. She looked down the length of the street.

There was no truck.

And there were no tracks in the freshly fallen snow!

CHAPTER 19

PACKAGES FROM AMERICA

Eventually, the supply of food brought home from Eschenrod ran out, and again the family went hungry. But God always provided. Faithful church members continued to pay their tithe in food items—a head of cabbage here, a few potatoes there.

Once Franz brought home a 100-pound bag of navy beans. How delicious they smelled when Helene cooked them! After she dished them into bowls, however, the children quickly lost their appetite when they noticed maggots floating on top. But in the end hunger won out. They scooped off the maggots and ate the rest.

Sometimes amid the dreariness there were bright spots. It was Lotte's job to walk the two miles to the Huegelstrasse every other day to buy the family's supply of milk.

One blustery day as she was fighting her way through a biting storm, an army jeep full of American soldiers roared by. Something hit her body. When she glanced up, she saw that the young GI's were waving to her. On the ground around her lay rolls of Lifesavers, the first she had ever seen. Delightedly she grabbed the colorful candy and hid it deep in her pocket.

Another time, early in the spring, Helene wanted to make a sauce to serve with oatmeal, so she sent Gerd to their leased garden plot to see if any of the rhubarb stalks were big enough to pick. Though he carefully looked the garden over, he saw only rhubarb sprouts.

Disconsolately, he was trudging back along the muddy path when he saw a lone American soldier standing in the field holding a huge brown paper bag. He beckoned to Gerd and put the bag into his arms. "Please take this to your mother right away," he said in fluent German. Dumbfounded, Gerd took the bag and staggered home with it.

Inside, the family discovered enough groceries to last a week: powdered eggs, powdered milk, butter, dried fruit, flour.

"Gerd, did you thank this man?"

"No, Mutti, I was too surprised to know what to say."

"Go back immediately and thank him. This is an answer to prayer."

Gerd went back, but even though he could see miles across the flat fields, there was no one there.

Some time later Helene sent Gerd to the basement to fetch potatoes for breakfast. Gerd carefully searched for anything edible. But the shelves were empty, the sacks lay limp. In one of the barrels he found a single small potato. Helene cut it into six slices and fried them for breakfast. One small slice of potato for each person.

That morning Franz spent an extra long time saying grace. He reminded God how He had provided throughout all the hard years and asked Him to continue to sustain the family. With growling stomachs the children waited for the interminable prayer to end.

Then Helene said, "Eat your food very slowly. God has given you 32 teeth so that you can chew each bite 32 times. If you eat slowly, the food is more filling." They ate slowly—but left the table hungry anyway.

The older children went to school. A little while later Franz got out his bicycle to make some pastoral visits.

"I'll be back at noon," he said, "so you can have lunch ready by then."

Helene rolled her eyes. "I will—if I have anything to fix. Remember, we're out of food!"

Helene spent the morning doing housework while Susi tagged along dusting and polishing the furniture. Helene's heart was heavy knowing the children would be starving by the time they came home from school.

At a quarter to 12, she decided that she would boil some water and put a little salt in it. *We'll just have to pretend it's soup,* she thought.

As she filled the kettle at the sink, she glanced out the kitchen window and noticed that the mail van had drawn up outside the house. Curiously Helene watched as the mailman got out a gigantic package. *I wonder who that's for?* she thought. Then she turned around and put the kettle on the burner.

At that moment the doorbell rang. Susi went to answer it, then came running back.

"Mutti, a man wants you."

Helene went to the door where the mailman handed her the delivery book to sign.

"Frau Hasel, I have a package from America for you. Please sign that you have received it."

"Oh," said Helene, disappointed. "If it's from America, it isn't for us. We don't know anybody there. It must be a mistake."

"It's for you," the mailman said. "Look. That's your address, isn't it?"

Helene bent over the brown wrapper. The address was in large block letters: *Familie Hasel, Frankfurt am Main, Nusszeil 97.* There could be no mistaking it. Mystified, she looked the package over. On the wrapping in bold red letters were the words: GIFT PARCEL. Helene's face blanched. She grabbed the doorframe for support. Gift in German means "poison."

Stunned, she said, "Why are they sending us a poison parcel from America? Who wants to destroy us now? I don't want this!"

The mailman smiled. "Frau Hasel, in English a gift is a present."

"Oh." Helene took a trembly breath. "Then I'll accept it."

In a daze she signed the delivery book, and heaved the heavy package onto the kitchen table. She cut the dirty string and tore the worn wrapping paper.

Out came a sturdy cardboard box filled with food! There was a bag of Pillsbury flour, a can of Crisco shortening, macaroni, powdered milk, powdered eggs, rice, sugar, dehydrated potatoes, cookies, soup mixes, nuts, dried California figs, and other fruit. A mysterious rustling bag turned out to be M&Ms. The table was piled high.

Helene felt her knees buckle. She quickly sat down.

"Thank you, Lord," she whispered fervently. "Why did I ever doubt you? A package from America! You have promised that even before we call you will answer. This package has traveled across the ocean for weeks, and we did not know then that we would need it so badly this very day. But You knew all along."

Now Helene jumped up. It was just a few minutes before noon. The salted water was already boiling. Quickly she dumped some macaroni in, and put some prunes to stew in another pot. Soon delicious smells wafted through the house.

The doorbell rang again—two short rings and one long one, the family signal. The children burst through the door.

"Oh, Mutti," they wailed. "We're so *hungry*. And somebody somewhere is cooking wonderful food!"

"Come into the kitchen," Helene said with a radiant smile. "I have a surprise for you."

Their eyes bulged when they saw the loaded kitchen table. Now they knew that it was their own meal they had smelled in the hallway outside. Soon all were seated around the table, and for the first time in weeks they all ate their fill.

After the meal the family wondered about the origins of this mysterious package. Carefully, they pieced the torn wrapping together and deciphered the return address. A name, a street in Lodi, California. They had never heard of Lodi, and knew no one there. Immediately they wrote a thank-you letter, telling about the parcel's mysterious and miraculous arrival.

Several months passed. No reply. Not realizing that Lodi has a large population of Germans, they decided that the sender probably couldn't understand German. So they wrote a second letter and had someone from the church translate it into English. After six months the letter came back, the torn, dirty envelope bearing a large red postal service stamp: RETURN TO SENDER. ADDRESSEE UNKNOWN. Who was the mysterious benefactor?

About a year after the enigmatic parcel, another package arrived from Lodi, California. This time the sender was someone named Lillian Bunch, who lived at a different address. In large letters it again bore the legend GIFT PARCEL.

In her panic, Helene forgot what the mailman had told her months before. "Stay away from this box," she shouted to the children, "or we'll all die!"

"Mutti, it's OK." Fortunately, Kurt had learned a few words of English in school and could reassure her. 'Gift' means it's a present."

"Oh. That's right." Relieved, Helene opened the package. Again there was food.

Again the Hasels composed a thank-you letter, and this time they got an answer. Once Lillian learned that the Hasels had 3-year-old Susi, she wrote back that she had a 3-year-old son, Tom. From that time on, she always included a small toy in the package of food. Once it was a set of tin doll dishes with Mickey Mouse on them. The children were intrigued but mystified—German kids knew nothing of Mickey Mouse.

Another time there were four jigsaw puzzles, each made up of seven large pieces. Time and again Susi would carefully put them together and then study the pictures: a pretty girl with blond curls in a frilly rose-red dress playing with a dollhouse, a freckled boy raking leaves into a tiny wheelbarrow in front of his white clapboard house. The scenes were exotic and unfamiliar—pictures of something Susi had never seen: a country not ravished by war.

Another package contained a three-inch-long baby doll, and another a strange utensil that had turning blades when you pushed it. Nobody could figure out what it was. Susi used it to pretend she was whipping cream or sharpening a pencil. Only when she came to America 15 years later did she discover its use: it was a toy hand-pushed lawnmower.

But the most marvelous thing of all was a small sky-blue sleigh with curved runners, intricate gingerbread decorations, and two yellow seats. A Saint Bernard was hitched to it by a red harness. And two tiny children were waving their hands as they gleefully glided along. The entire toy fit into the palm of Susi's small hand.

For several years, Lillian's packages arrived at regular intervals, always containing the most essential food items. In addition to Susi's toy, there were other treats—a Hershey chocolate bar or a bag of hard candy. Sometimes the food was puzzling, like the jar filled with a thick brown paste. Lotte tried to eat a spoonful and discovered that while it tasted good, it stuck to her mouth. That was the Hasels' introduction to peanut butter.

As the years went by and the country recovered from the war, starvation was no longer a constant threat. Now 6, Susi was just getting ready to start school when she caught whooping cough. Day and night she was racked by spasms of coughing that made it impossible for her to breathe. For weeks she had the terrifying feeling that she was going to suffocate, and Mother and Lotte took turns sitting by her bed and wiping the sweat off her blue little face.

Finally, she recovered, and Helene laid out the clothes she'd need for school. During her daughter's illness she'd washed and ironed Susi's few clothes, and now she tried them on her.

"Oh, horror," she gulped. "Lotte, look. Susi outgrew her clothes while she was sick!"

"School starts tomorrow," Lotte said. "What are we going to do?"

That afternoon another package arrived from Lillian Bunch. These were always red-letter days, and again the whole family gathered around and waited eagerly for the string to be cut. As the wrapping paper fell away, there arose the now-familiar smell they associated with America.

When the flaps were folded back, everybody gasped in surprise. For the first time in three years, the box contained no food. Instead it was filled with dresses for a 6-year-old girl: a blue and white striped dress with a white bib, a plaid dress with ruffles and puffed sleeves, a red polka dot that tied in the back. Each dress was exquisite. These were clothes like the girls in the puzzle pictures wore. No one in Germany owned anything so beautiful.

Round-eyed, Susi watched as the marvelous carton was unpacked. At the very bottom there appeared a small red button-up cardigan.

This red sweater immediately caught Susi's fancy. Of all the clothes she owned, she loved it the most. She wore it until the elbows were worn through and Helene had to cut the sleeves off and make it into a short-sleeved sweater. It served for another year. By that time it had grown too small and was very shabby. Still, no matter how much Helene coaxed and pleaded, Susi could not be persuaded to get rid of it.

Then, one day, it disappeared. When Susi woke up in the morning, the sweater had simply vanished.

"Kurt, Gerd, Lotte, Mutti, have you seen my sweater?"

They just shrugged their shoulders. Disconsolately, Susi ran from room to room and searched the wardrobes and drawers. There was no sign of the red sweater. Finally she realized that it was gone for good. She didn't talk about it much anymore, but she remembered.

Fall came, then winter. Finally, it was Christmas. Under the tree was a small gift for everyone. But hidden way in the back stood a box for Susi. Eagerly she wanted to tear the paper off, but Papa Franz said, "Slow down. Don't tear the paper or the ribbon. Open the wrappings carefully so we can use them again."

Painstakingly, her small fingers peeled away the wrappings. Finally the lid came off. Susi took one look inside and squealed with delight. There was an entire outfit for her baby doll. A hat, a scarf, mittens, a sweater, and pants. Mother had carefully cut her red sweater apart and remade it into doll garments. Susi was thrilled. Now she could keep her red sweater forever.

Many years later after Susi had immigrated to the United States and settled at Pacific Union College in Angwin, California, she learned that Lodi was not too far away. She contacted the pastor there and arranged to visit the church on a Sabbath morning. She told the story of that miraculous first parcel of food in the hopes a church member would remember having sent it. No one did. At that point Susi didn't remember Lillian Bunch's name, and Lillian wasn't present that Sabbath and therefore didn't hear Susi's story.

Several years later, Susi received a phone call at work.

"My name is Lillian Bunch," the voice on the other end said. "I sent packages to your family after the war."

"Oh," Susi cried, "how did you find me? I have been looking for you for years!"

The two women arranged to meet, and Lillian came to Angwin to visit Susi. She told a strange story. She and her sister were planning a trip to Germany. Lillian remembered the Hasel family and wondered if she could locate any of them. She looked up the name in the *Seventh-day Adventist Yearbook* and found Kurt Hasel listed as a pastor in Germany. Recognizing that he was one of the children, she wrote to him and asked to visit him. He, in turn, told her that his sister lived at Pacific Union College.

Now, finally, Susi was able to tell her benefactor how Lillian's generous packages had literally kept the Hasel family alive. She showed Lillian the little blue sleigh and the doll clothes made from the sweater— gifts she had treasured for 30 years and brought with her to America. The two women embraced, both of them crying.

"How did you come to send packages to us in the first place?" Susi asked when she had dried her tears.

"I heard about the terrible poverty in Germany," Lillian said. "I was a mother with young children then, and my heart went out to the German people. I wanted to help some family in need, so I went to my pastor. Together we picked a name out of the *SDA Yearbook,* and it was your father's."

"When did you start sending us parcels?"

"In 1947."

That meant that someone else had sent that very first package since it had arrived a whole year before. Lillian knew nothing about it. Where had it come from?

CHAPTER 20

AFTERMATH

By the fall of 1945 it was abundantly clear that though the war was over, prejudice against Sabbath keepers was not. Kurt, who was now attending the Gymnasium, the German equivalent to high school, came home time and again with reports of discrimination.

"The teachers are scheduling all tests on Sabbath so that I will miss them. They won't let me make them up," he complained.

Another time it was "They won't let me participate in the speech contest because I was not in class on Sabbath."

Every week there were new grievances while Kurt's grades plummeted.

Because of the Sabbath problems, Franz and Helene had already decided earlier that they would not send Lotte to the Gymnasium but would let her finish only the compulsory eight grades of elementary school. Now they made up their minds to take Kurt out of school also and apprentice him to learn a trade, knowing that without completion of the Gymnasium, he would never be able to attend university.

At 8:00 one morning Franz went to the courthouse downtown where the employment agency was located—to search for an apprenticeship for his son.

As he walked upstairs he heard someone call out, "Franz, Franz!"

The voice sounded familiar, but in the dark corridor Franz couldn't be sure who it was. Then he saw a man sitting on the bench—Lieutenant Gutschalk, Peter Gutschalk.

"Peter, what are you doing here?"

"I have to go in there," Peter replied, jerking his head in the direction of a nearby courtroom.

"What's happening?"

"It's an American military tribunal that is bringing all Nazis to trial."

"I am really interested in that whole process," Franz said. "When I am done upstairs, I'll come and listen in."

Franz was delighted to discover that a horticulture apprenticeship was available. It was ideal for Kurt, who loved nature and all living things, and it was close enough to the apartment that Kurt could bike home for lunch every day. Breathing a prayer of gratitude, Franz left.

Downstairs, court was already in session. Franz—the only civilian spectator—took a seat in the back row. As he took his seat, he heard the judge read the list of accusations against Peter Gutschalk. Franz marveled at how many details the judge knew. Even before the war had started, Peter had been a concentration camp guard accused of unusual cruelty. Later he participated in the Kristallnacht, November 8, 1938, a night of persecution against the Jews that got its name for all the broken shop window glass. In less than 20 hours, $23 million worth of damage was done.

To each charge, Gutschalk replied flatly, "I don't know anything about that. I have no memory of that."

Speechless, Franz shook his head. In the army Gutschalk had often bragged about his exploits. On the Kristallnacht he had personally led a detachment of Nazis that burned down a Jewish synagogue.

The judge, who would have none of this memory loss, knew many details about this event. He knew the make of the truck Gutschalk had ridden in, and the exact time of the incident, because the truck driver had testified against him. Citing the details, the judge said, "Herr Gutschalk, I want you to tell me what you did during those 15 minutes."

Again Gutschalk said, "I cannot remember anything!"

Meanwhile the bailiff stepped up to Franz.

"I see you shaking your head. Do you know this man?"

"Oh yes," said Franz. "I know him very well. I am just surprised that he doesn't remember anything. We were together during the war, and he told us many stories."

"Would you be willing to serve as a witness?"

"No, sir. I am a Christian. I won't testify against him."

The trial lasted until 11:00. In disgust, the judge said to Gutschalk, "You remind me of a worker in the Adler motorcycle plant. He had stolen a motor and, carrying it on his shoulder, was ready to walk out the gate when he was stopped and questioned by the guard.

"'What do you have on your shoulder?'

"'What? Where?'

"'Here on your shoulder. You're carrying a motor!'

"'I don't know anything about that. Someone must have loaded it onto my shoulder when I wasn't paying attention!'"

Turning to Gutschalk, the judge continued, "That's how you strike me! Now I will give you one week. If in that time you can't find any witnesses that can vouch for your innocence during those 15 minutes, you are done for. Court is adjourned!"

Franz and Gutschalk walked out together.

"Peter," Franz said, "how can you lie like that? You bragged to us about killing Jews and destroying stores and the synagogue in Frankfurt. And remember the Jew in the Ukraine that I pulled out of the pit? If I had told everything I know, you would go to prison now. All during the war, you were my enemy and tried to do me in because I am a Christian. Now, my Christianity is your salvation. Because of it, I remained silent rather than testify against you."

On the steps the men parted. Franz never learned what became of Lieutenant Gutschalk.

Franz got word that his friend Karl had also been released. Karl lived across from the Adventist church in Frankfurt, so every Friday night before vespers, Franz visited him. One evening, Karl came to the door very worked up.

"Franz, I got a letter from Hauptmann Miekus. In order to be employed again as a professor of history, he needs an affidavit stating that he committed no war crimes. Remember how he wanted to shoot me in 1942 because I said we had already lost the war? I am not going to write any such thing. He always had it in for me. The very nerve!"

Silently, Franz listened while making his own plans. The following week he visited their mutual friend, Willi, and casually asked for the Hauptmann's address in the town of Lahn. Then he wrote his own affidavit. He gave his own credentials: name, birthdate, birthplace, the fact he had never been a party member, the fact that he was a pastor in the Seventh-day Adventist Church.

He continued, "Even though Mr. Miekus was a committed member of the National Socialist German Worker's Party, he was a team player who would have gone through fire for us." Then he recounted the time Miekus had let a soldier off the hook who had been drunk on guard duty, how he had saved the soldier who had talked about defecting to the enemy, how he had saved Franz when Franz said Hitler was a scoundrel, and many other incidents. He sent this document with a cover letter to Hauptmann Miekus.

Three days later Franz received a response: "Dear Comrade Hasel! Please allow me to call you that. I never had any idea you were not a party member. Please accept my sincerest appreciation for your document!" As a result of this affidavit, Professor Miekus was acquitted and allowed to teach again.

One Sabbath in 1953 Franz was preaching in the town of Lahn. Afterward, the church elder, a dentist, invited him home for dinner.

"I can't stay very long," Franz explained. "My old Hauptmann lives somewhere around here, and I want to visit him."

"Oh," the dentist said, "who is it? I know everybody."

"His name is Miekus."

"I am sorry to tell you this, but Professor Miekus died last year."

"I am sad to hear that," Franz said. "Let me tell you a little about him." He recounted some of his war experiences with the Hauptmann, and told how he'd given the officer a Bible study on the image in Daniel, and how Miekus had borrowed his Bible.

With growing interest in his eyes, the dentist followed the story. When Franz finished, he nodded his head.

"Now," he said, "I understand something that has puzzled me for years. I don't know if you realized it when you served with him, but Miekus was a Catholic. You remember how Catholics created so many difficulties for Adventist children who didn't attend school on Sabbath. Well, every one of my children had Miekus for a teacher. He always gave them their Sabbaths off, and he never, ever scheduled tests on Sabbath. I often wondered why, but now I see. I am so grateful that all my children were able to finish the Gymnasium."

Before Franz left, the family formed a circle and prayed. Together they thanked God for His guiding hand through all of their lives.

On the way home Franz reflected on what he had heard. *Lord, you prepared a way for these children to get an education, but the door seems closed to my own. What would You have us do?*

The decision to send a child to the Gymnasium has to be made at the end of fourth grade. It was time to decide for Gerd. The family gathered one evening in the living room for worship.

"Gerd," Franz began. "You remember the trouble Kurt had in the Gymnasium. I have made inquiries and have learned that his old teachers are still there. From other Adventists I know that in order to succeed one needs to attend school on Sabbath." Franz pulled out his handkerchief and blew his nose noisily. "I know how you love learning," he continued. "You would like to study at a university. If we don't send you to the Gymnasium you will not have this opportunity. What do you want to do?"

Everyone's eyes were on Gerd as he swallowed hard. Then, without hesitation, he said, "Papa, I don't want to go through what Kurt went through. And I want to keep the Commandments. I will stay in elementary school and do an apprenticeship."

Helene put her arms around Gerd and held him tight. She understood the sacrifice he was making.

Then the family knelt together while Franz prayed. "Lord, all through the war You protected us and, in the end, brought us back together safely. Now Gerd has decided to be faithful in Sabbathkeeping rather than get a higher education. I pray that you will not let this be a disadvantage to him as he prepares to work for You."

The family rose, formed a circle, and once again sang their favorite hymn:

"A mighty fortress is our God . . .

"We will not fear, for God hath willed
His truth to triumph through us . . .

"The body they may kill; God's truth abideth still,
His Kingdom is forever."

EPILOGUE

Franz served as a pastor in the Frankfurt area until the publishing work resumed in 1950. He eventually became publishing secretary for the Central European Division. In addition to his work, he chose to visit every Adventist church in Germany on a rotating basis and preach the Sabbath sermon. After his retirement in 1965, he continued to colporteur with the aim of finding people with whom to study the Bible. This he continued doing until he died at age 92. As a result of his work many were baptized. At the end of his life he had read the Bible through 89 times. Many young people whom he had befriended attended his funeral. One of them summarized the loss they felt by asking disconsolately, "Who will pray for us now?"

Helene developed rheumatoid arthritis following the war. She suffered pain until she died at age 82. During the last 20 years of her life she was so crippled that she was bedridden. She often questioned why God allowed her suffering. It was not until after she was anointed, according to the injunction in James 5, that she accepted her illness and was able to find peace. During those last 20 years she wrote more than 2,000 poems.

Kurt finished his horticulture apprenticeship, then went to the Marienhoehe Seminary and took the ministerial course. He attended Newbold College for a year, then became a pastor and evangelist in Germany. He is retired and lives in southern Germany. He is still active in conducting spiritual emphasis seminars. Kurt and his wife, Berbel, have three children: Frank, Jutta, and Bettina. Frank completed a Ph.D. at Andrews University and is part of the theology faculty at Bogenhofen Adventist Seminary in Austria. Jutta is a nurse. She is at home, raising her two young children. Bettina lives with her husband in Bern, where she works as a secretary for the Euro-Africa Division.

Liselotte (Lotte) married an American serviceman and immigrated to the United States. Until her retirement, she worked in the Home Health Education Service Office of the Pacific Union Conference. She lives in southern California. She and her husband, William, have two children: Tedd and Susan. Tedd is a physical therapist, and Susan is a church school teacher.

Gerhard (Gerd) finished an electrician apprenticeship, then went to the Marienhoehe Seminary and took the ministerial course. Unable to go to a university in Germany, he came to the United States to complete his education at Atlantic Union College, Andrews University, and Vanderbilt University, where he received his Ph.D. For many years he was a professor and dean at the Seventh-day Adventist Theological Seminary at Andrews University in Berrien Springs, Michigan, and was an internationally renowned Old Testament scholar. He published 14 books and more than 300 articles. He was killed in a car accident in 1994. His favorite hymn, "A Mighty Fortress Is Our God," was performed at his funeral. His wife, Hilde, still lives in Berrien Springs, Michigan, where she teaches church school. They have three children: Michael, Marlena, and Melissa. Michael received a Ph.D. from the University of Arizona. He is part of the theology faculty at Southern Adventist University in Tennessee. Marlena is a dietitian. Melissa is a church school teacher.

Susi studied for two years at Newbold College. When Gerhard received a call to teach at Southern Missionary College (now Southern Adventist University) in Tennessee, he invited her to join him and Hilde there to complete her education. At SMC she met and married her husband, Bill. Since 1975, she and her family have been at Pacific Union College, where Bill is a professor of physics. Susi earned an M.A. degree in clinical psychology and is a licensed marriage, family, and child therapist. She did private practice counseling for 10 years. When she became registrar at Pacific Union College in California in 1993, she learned that Lillian Bunch's son, Tom, was registrar at Southwestern Adventist College (now Southwestern Adventist University) in Texas. She has spent four summers in Russia conducting evangelistic meetings for children. She and Bill have two children: Rico and Marcus. Rico works in the computer center at Pacific Union College. Marcus is a physical therapy assistant.